SHOW, DON'T TELL

SHOW, DON'T TELL

A WRITER, HER TEACHER, AND THE POWER OF SHARING OUR STORIES

KRISTINE GASBARRE

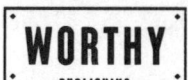

WORTHY
· PUBLISHING ·

New York   Nashville

Worthy

Hachette Book Group

1290 Avenue of the Americas, New York, NY 10104

worthypublishing.com

@WorthyPub

First Edition: April 2025

Worthy is a division of Hachette Book Group, Inc. The Worthy name and logo are registered trademarks of Hachette Book Group, Inc.

The publisher is not responsible for websites (or their content) that are not owned by the publisher.

The Hachette Speakers Bureau provides a wide range of authors for speaking events. To find out more, go to hachettespeakersbureau.com or email HachetteSpeakers@hbgusa.com.

Worthy Books may be purchased in bulk for business, educational, or promotional use. For information, please contact your local bookseller or the Hachette Book Group Special Markets Department at special.markets@hbgusa.com.

Print book interior design by Amy Quinn

Library of Congress Cataloging-in-Publication Data

Names: Gasbarre, Kristine, author.

Title: Show, don't tell : a writer, her teacher, and the power of sharing our stories / Kristine Gasbarre.

Description: First edition. | New York : Worthy, [2025]

Identifiers: LCCN 2024051616 | ISBN 9781546008064 (hardcover) | ISBN 9781546008088 (ebook)

Subjects: LCSH: Korthaus, Carol, 1941-. | Women teachers—United States—Biography. | Gasbarre, Kristine. | Women authors—United States—Biography. | Teacher-student relationships—United States. | Teachers—Conduct of life. | Self-actualization (Psychology) | Women in education—United States—Social conditions.

Classification: LCC LA2311.K67 G37 2025 | DDC 373.110092 [B]—dc23/eng/20250122

LC record available at https://lccn.loc.gov/2024051616

ISBNs: 9781546008064 (hardcover), 9781546008088 (ebook)

Printed in Canada

MRQ

Printing 1, 2025

In loving memory of Lisa Graffius Blasdell.

Miss Graffius,
your laughter has been the most lasting
part of the lesson.

Whatever you choose to do, leave tracks. That means don't do it just for yourself. You will want to leave the world a little better for your having lived.

—**Justice Ruth Bader Ginsburg**

No matter what accomplishments you make, somebody helped you.

—**Althea Gibson**

CONTENTS

TEACH THE WHOLE PERSON

"Sauvignon Blanc?"

When I glance up from my menu, staring back at me is a black skull that rises out of the V-neck of her country club golf uniform. I clock that this emblem definitely *wasn't* on my favorite waitress's chest last week.

I shift my gaze and smile back. "Like always," I respond, willing myself not to study the artwork that covers her collarbone.

I'm mildly dazed as she walks away. Part of the reason I find myself measuring the glaring scale of her decision—I mean, the *size* of that tattoo—is that I can take a pretty decent guess at why she did it: probably to get some guy's attention.

Twenty years ago, I'd been that young woman: a girl with the subtlest sense that the future has big things in store but who is too scared to leave what she knows, while not yet stocked with enough confidence to believe she's cut out for more. In my upbringing, I'd been taught that in the eyes of our Creator, each one of us is a treasure.

But in our town, I'd learned that a woman is worth only as much as she believes she is.

A small town has a way of making a girl's whole world small. When it came time to decide where to go next and what to do for the rest of my life, I found it tough to imagine what was "out there," and even tougher to know what was *inside*. Of me.

Sure, I performed well in school, but I wasn't genuinely invested in my potential—in fact, I feared success. A *career* seemed scary. If I'd had my way back then, I'd have chosen to stay right where I was for the rest of my life.

It was a blessing that I didn't get my way. One woman had an important part in that.

I was fourteen when I met that firecracker of a soul, a bombastic professor of life with colossal charisma who, meanwhile, stood all of four foot ten. She was different— and she was present throughout those teen years, patiently and persistently drawing out proof of my capabilities. She gave me an unjudged ground to tumble through young mistakes and learn, by trial and error, who I wanted to become—who I *could* become.

In time, that would also lead me to appreciate who she would become to me.

Just like an artist uses paint for her or his canvas, a teacher has chosen children as her or his medium. No amount of effort, time, patience, prayers, or money is lost on the cause of children.

—Mrs. Shick, elementary teacher in rural Pennsylvania

INTRODUCTION

THE CHARACTER

"Now, that's something!"

I and several other patrons turn our heads toward Mrs. Korthaus's raspy roar as she enters the country club and audibly admires the artwork our waitress is newly exhibiting. Her raucous energy is balanced by her sweater vest and golf skirt, her one-of-a-kind, chaotic yet composed brand of brilliance.

"Sorry I'm a minute late," my old high school teacher says as she brushes the wind out of her bangs and shimmies into the wooden booth. "The breast cancer golf benefit is next week, and our planning meeting ran over."

"For the first time in history, you're not the one waiting on me."

"Did you *know*," she says, characteristically giving the final consonant its own syllable for dramatic emphasis, "ten of us playing this year are cancer survivors?"

Mrs. Korthaus is eighty-two years old and battling breast cancer as we speak. But nothing, not even cancer, can stop her from giving her time and energy.

"Ah," she sighs, resting her elbows on the table, one

hand covering the other fist in the same contented way I've known her to do for more than two decades. I love to study her hands, small but strong, her nails characteristically blunt and bare. To me they've always represented a life active and occupied, the hands of a woman who's forever on the move enjoying her life.

Even the pronunciation of her husband's German last name, *courthouse*, personifies—to use a term she taught me—some of her own traits. Sturdy and solid, always fearless to stand for what's right. Famously fair in her understanding, and generous in granting the benefit of the doubt.

And, she's funny. If Judge Judy taught Shakespearean comedy or Dr. Ruth coached the golf team, then you can imagine Mrs. Korthaus. She's known for her chiseled cheekbones and plainspoken thoughts, her larger-than-life, exclamatory mannerisms, and a joy-filled spirit like Oprah's old holiday gift giveaway episodes: *YOU get an A, and YOU get an A!* Her students went to her when we were applying to college, seeking the kind of teacher who gave a thoughtful recommendation letter. Our reliance on her was a testament to her gift for helping us see the good in ourselves when we hadn't yet learned to find it in the mirror.

As much as she had taught me about literary works and approaches to journalism, knowledge I took heedfully into my career, I'd also studied the way she made the world better and herself, happy. I was captivated to witness this brave woman use her voice, gritty and forthright. I'd never known a female so self-propelled. A lot of the women in our town, and in both her family and mine, had been largely in the background, not at the table where decisions were being made. Mrs. Korthaus now sighs at their preoccupation with appearances—"With their wardrobes! And their jewelry! And their big, ridiculous houses!" (To be fair, she used a far more flavorful adjective than "ridiculous." Her impulse to mince no words is one of her traits I love the most.) Her point is that a woman will be confused about what makes her worthy if she's never had to stretch and discover her own capabilities to support herself.

We were both raised in places led by men where the women were fiercely loyal at following males' leads—from the sports teams we supported to the presidents we voted for. Growing up, I hadn't seen a woman try to hold her own in a business meeting, but I'd seen them exchange choice words when one got a nicer car, or when one's husband advanced at work. The unmarried ones were typically nuns or widows, and for the rest, the last name of the man she'd marry seemed more important than the one she was capable of making for herself. *Behind every great man is a great woman!* Behind every successful child was also a devoted mom: The accomplishments of her children were considered her own greatest accomplishments.

MRS. KORTHAUS MADE HER CLASSES ABOUT WRITING, literature, and communications a window to the world for a school full of kids unaware of how sheltered our rural roots had made us. The multiple extracurricular activities she helmed showed us a woman fulfilled by her passions. Sitting in her classroom, the perceptive student might sense that she had carved out some space in her early life to explore her values and her identity. Even if we didn't fully grasp it at the time, we could imagine that before she became our teacher, her life had been full of curiosity and adventure. We could have asked her to share her stories, but most of us hadn't yet learned the thoughtful and courageous skill of asking questions.

Standing on a chair to make her point (and, I suspect, for a full view of the classroom), she'd cry, "The hu-*MAN*-uh-teez!" as her pointer finger poked holes in the thin air above her, like Braveheart rallying his troops before the Battle of Stirling. To her, the humanities were those subjects that showed the dignity and goodness within every human, the inherent need to feel a sense of worth—in ourselves and in others.

She didn't have to demand that we listen; she inspired us to pay attention with the way she radiated her joy of learning.

In her classroom, a thin wood podium and a backless metal stool stood front and center. She would sit comfortably, legs crossed and hands folded over her knee, facing us as she read a passage from a work she'd just discovered or rediscovered. She was known for jumping off the stool and frantically searching every surface of her desk for her reading glasses...which were usually nestled on top of her head. When one of us said something mischievous as she paced between rows, she'd pop onto her tiptoes and clutch her chest, howling sharply as if we were giving her a heart attack. Instead of reprimanding our teenage antics, Mrs. Korthaus often played along. On rare occasions, she'd curse in class, trusting our young adulthood to hear her with maturity. "Well, what the hell, you guys? Isn't anybody gonna take a stab at an answer?"

"*Carol…*," one of the boys might playfully growl in response. These small things, especially in a Catholic school as disciplined as ours, felt like unspoken pacts reinforcing our trust in her—reminding us that she saw us as equals. Calling a teacher by her first name was one of the ultimate acts of pushing one's luck, but she'd carry on merrily with the lesson, assuring us we were safe.

In her eyes, the only behavior that called for discipline was failing to stretch the farthest we could. Yet she understood that "stretching" meant something different for everyone. She was committed to noticing every student—really seeing each of us—which is why so many thrived in her classes and beyond. She knew that a child's behavior reveals the difference between one who feels loved and one who doesn't.

All this is why, about two decades since I'd sat in her classroom, after I had moved away for a writing career then moved again, I'm sitting in this country club. I'm taking this rare chance to re-embrace her in my life. Our friendship is an *elective* commitment, as they say in academia. Non-obligatory, like all the most precious commitments we choose to keep. I still think of myself as her student, and she remains my most understanding confidante.

"That tattoo," I whisper. "Didn't she just recently tell us she's looking for an office job to support her son? I was thinking of introductions we could make for her..."

"We make our own decisions in life," she says, gesturing an exchange with the waitress, who's already caught the message to pour her Chardonnay, "and we learn from the outcome whether they were good decisions or poor decisions." A classic Korthaus-ism.

"Mrs. Korthaus." I lean in with a whisper.

"You know you can call me Carol."

"No, I can't," I tell her. She's been saying this since graduation day, but it would feel like calling a grandparent by their first name. "Listen: *The tattoo is bigger than she is*. What would we call that, a metaphor?"

"A comparison," she says.

As if to punctuate her answer, our waitress returns and places a glass in front of her. In an instant, Mrs. Korthaus has struck up a conversation about the new ink job with examination and intrigue, as though the two of them were standing side by side admiring a Van Gogh at the Met.

Of everything I have ever loved about her, this moment is the ultimate example. Just when it's wildly possible you've made the worst mistake of your life, Mrs. Korthaus responds with openness instead of judgment. There is no dwelling, there is no looking down upon, there is no lecturing. If you've paid attention to her lessons over the years—and especially if you've watched her—then you've learned to live with your decisions, and you're making the best of every outcome. In a moment when most adults would turn their backs on you, Mrs. Korthaus leans in and engages: *Tell me more...*

This time around, I've asked her to tell *me* more, to revisit all I didn't understand in my young years about her faith in how far my life could take me. I had achieved things that, when I first met her, I hadn't the imagination, let alone the audacity, to dream. Now, our experience of discussing life as women together was becoming something of a story of its own. In a world of dizzying standards for women, I couldn't help but wonder: Had I lived up to the ones my most enduring mentor had instilled in me?

At age thirty-five, after I've achieved what she'd once told me I could—and, now, bought a house on my own back in my hometown—I recognize what a gift it is to spend time all these years later with my favorite teacher and how rare this chance is to gain a glimpse inside the life of the woman who shaped my own life so significantly. The possibility for me to become self-sufficient started in her classroom. Then Mrs. Korthaus continued with me on my journey, nudging me to try things I'd once barely had the guts or imagination to dream.

I'd learned so much from her that I asked Mrs. Korthaus if she'd join me in writing a book.

"Us?" she said. "Together?"

I nodded.

"A book."

I laughed. "*Yes.*"

Our discussions take place at her kitchen table or as we walk along the lake where we were neighbors when I was growing up and are once again. Instead of standing at the chalkboard, she stands over the stove making us one of her generous four-course dinners, or we meet for a dinner date to catch the happy hour specials at our country club by the lake.

The only challenge has been that one of us is used to working on serious deadlines. The other, let's just say, is a lot more accustomed to assigning them. She leaves me no choice but to contend with her schedule, since even in her eighties she's the only person more involved in high school extracurriculars than I was in the late 1990s. Interviews for this project were often timed around her schedule coaching the mock trial team, meeting with the journalism club, and helping out with the spring musical. "Want to have a glass of wine and catch up tomorrow night?" I ask as we pass each other walking our dogs.

"Can't!" she calls back at me over her shoulder. "I've got bridge!"

"I've been calling your house. I was worried."

"Gee whiz, I forgot to tell you: I got rid of my landline! Didn't need it anymore!"

When I text her, it often takes a couple days for her to text back. **Sorry!!** she finally responds. **I was busy following the baseball team around. Can you believe it? STATE CHAMPS! First time since your brother's old team!**

My heavens, her memory. It had been twenty-two years since my brother and his team won the state title.

For years she coached tennis and led the National Honor Society and some of the school's programs in spiritual life. She helped launch the school system's inaugural 1990s CARE Team in response to students' mental health needs, decades before society recognized that we needed the world inside our minds to be as healthy as our bodies. She emceed the annual spring auction since the kickoff year in 1992 when she'd famously sipped one too many Chardonnays and once or twice ended up awarding the big-ticket prizes to the wrong bidders. Nobody minded— after all, she was the entertainment everyone came to see. The morning after the auction, she'd meet the prom committee to help set up decorations.

But once she started to focus on her work, I started to witness how profound our moments were becoming for her. On one occasion, I arrive at her house to find a yellow legal pad filled top to bottom in her expressive, abstract handwriting that resembles Keith Haring's art more than the prudent, lacy cursive both my grandmas used to use. I flip the pages, discovering some of her memories, thoughts from old lesson plans, and "Korthaus-isms," as we called them back then: *You can do anything with a degree in the humanities!* or, *Expose self to every facet of professional life! Travel! Then take a deep breath.*

At another point, she hands me a file folder, inside which I find a small stack of single-spaced pages. At the top, I read:

BECAUSE YOU ASKED.

Born 8/23/41, the first child of Mary Nanni and Tony Persichetti…

She's documented her life story for me. "How long did this take you?"

She shrugs. "A few days." *Bless her.* "It was no big deal," she quickly adds, now searching her wet bar for a corkscrew. "We had a couple snow days. I needed something to do."

As the journalist I am, I record our conversations on audio. Like the English student I used to be, I also take down notes in a ferocious attempt to capture the essence of her wisdom. This time around, she filters nothing, and the secrets and events she shares reveal an even deeper power in the woman I thought I knew. While she was encouraging us to tell our stories, she was brimming with so many of her own. She reveals her life in chapters: a season for education; a season for work; a season for family; the season she calls her "comfort zone," when she enjoyed the blend of marriage and career; the season after her husband dies, which she dedicates to her faith—and her love for her friends woven into every one. All these experiences contributed to her growth—"lifelong learning," she still calls it—and this reminds me of one of my favorite phrases: *Goodness is its own reward*. The love of learning is self-rewarding.

It's a treat that after a visit with her I can wander home on foot to the quiet cabin I've bought, not far from where she still lives in the bright, well-kept one-story on the lake, the place a group of us theater kids used to house-sit when she and her husband traveled in the summers. She trusted us *that* much.

"Do you remember?" I ask her one night. "The summer going into our junior year, we found the book that you kept on your nightstand: *Is It Hot in Here, or Is It Me?*"

"HA!" she exclaims. Her famous *crack* of a laugh. Her generation kept "the change of life" private—but not her. To me, that book about menopause that lay within easy reach of her pillow proved that she hadn't wanted to stash that personal detail away from us, even though she knew that we would snoop through the house. I remember standing there, looking at the book and admiring her for her determination to research the answers she needed for her health. It also occurred to me that her husband must have loved and accepted her through all those changes.

She taught us about foreshadowing as a literary device, and that book on the nightstand had been an example of it. With so many challenges women face, Mrs. Korthaus had foreshadowed for me an example of what to do—if I put my mind to it, I could figure out how to overcome just about any obstacle in my life.

I'D DEMONSTRATED TO MYSELF THAT I WAS, IN FACT, CAPABLE of what Mrs. Korthaus had long ago jockeyed for me just to try. I'd worked for a couple of the biggest publishers and media companies in the world. I'd lived internationally and spent a decade working in New York City. I'd written a *New York Times* bestseller. I'd been on Oprah's TV network—I mean, I used to race home from the bus stop to pour a bowl of cereal and watch Oprah at four o'clock every afternoon.

I'd followed the call into a profession that deserved its reputation for being tough, and I'd sacrificed meeting a partner or starting a family: two dreams that had never gone away but hadn't come to fruition. So when I started searching to buy a house, it didn't take me long to realize that my longings to be close to nature, my family, and my familiar roots would make my hometown the most sensible place to settle down. It was also a budget-friendly market for me to join the growing demographic of single female first-time homebuyers.

I hadn't quite expected to find that back home, the opinions about women's roles hadn't budged much since I first entered Mrs. Korthaus's classroom over twenty years ago. Some people were suspicious of this mature but unsettled-down version of me—a young woman who'd once been reluctant to live outside of town, who'd originally wanted nothing more than to get married, have kids, and stay local. In my years living away, though, I'd managed to become so uninterested in those conventions, I was getting the impression that to some neighbors, I couldn't be trusted. I was a writer who believed women should determine our own futures and was critical about what hadn't worked well for us in the past. Free-spirited, self-supporting, and perfectly delighted with all of the above.

"You've come back here?" one of my grade school teachers asked me at a picnic. "Are you...*happy*?"

"She's lived here her whole entire life," I later vented to Mrs. Korthaus. "Is *she* happy?"

Mrs. Korthaus replied with the philosophical mindset that led me to become the thinker I am today. "Even if we give every student the best possible chance to have professional success: What is really a well-educated person? Or a truly happy person?"

SHE'D TAUGHT ME THE ART OF THE RHETORICAL QUESTION, and in our time together, she's asked me a few doozies. Some made her my antagonist, just like in the literature she long ago introduced to me, as she provoked me and continued to call out my long-held notions about what I thought my life should look like.

But aside from our deep inquiries, a part of me had just missed her. When someone we love passes away, we're typically left to dwell on not having spent enough time with them. But what about the rare soul with whom we find ourselves treasuring bonus time at a stage in life when we weren't bold enough to hope for it—when now we can grasp how meaningful it is?

I began incorporating a weekly STEAM challenge into my third-grade classroom. Students are placed into small groups, given random materials, and instructed to create something to solve a specific problem. My female students beam with pride when their builds impress and often surpass the creativity of their male peers. After the first few weeks, one little girl announced to her friends that she now wants to be an engineer. When I asked what inspired her to persevere on a particularly difficult build, she boldly told me, "I started working harder when I believed I was smarter than I ever believed before."

—Ms. Tilson, elementary teacher in Colorado

CHAPTER ONE

THE OBJECTIVE

WHEN I WAS A STRUGGLING TEENAGER, MRS. KORTHAUS was often one of the very few who'd really seen and encouraged my writing. I'd come to believe in her perception of my skill because she had been out in the world. As her student, writing for an assignment, I'd reveal my feelings to her—just her. Then, in my early twenties, I finally felt courageous enough to try to get published. She'd taught us how every main character, every protagonist, has a motivation—an objective. In class, we watched *Citizen Kane*—Charles Foster Kane's quest for power and success provides exposition to the viewer that reveals how finite our chance is to ask someone the big questions about their life. She taught us classical Greek drama, like *Oedipus Rex*, in which Oedipus tries to flee the fate that an oracle says has been predestined for him.

"Hubris!" she cries out, referencing Oedipus's tragic flaw that ironically resulted in his death: the very fate he was trying to avoid. "Ooh," she says, with a shudder of satisfaction. "That's still one of my favorite words."

It's this desire to spread her passion for learning and seizing life's experiences that still drives her every day. At age eighty-one, when she finally decides to hang up her weathered Central Catholic Cardinals tote and leave full-time teaching, it's not because of her age—for several years, she's said, "Friends keep asking me when I'm going to retire!"—but it's as though that notion hadn't even made it onto her radar. Her departure also wasn't because her husband died; in fact, that gave her even more reason to fill her days with work. It isn't even because post-pandemic education had increasingly asked educators to teach students through a screen, which she loathes. "And I don't want to learn new technology!" she says, unabashedly. The power of learning from her was sitting in her classroom, not from expecting her to shuffle a mouse around and click through slides. When she finally retires, it's not even because of the sound of blanks being fired during active shooter drills where she and all the teachers at our K–12 alma mater cover the windows and block the doors and direct students into designated hiding places with their "safety buckets" full of first aid supplies. If anything, protecting young minds would have kept her working forever.

Retiring is also not because of the breast cancer. Anytime I ask how she's feeling, or how the week's appointment went with her oncologist, or how the oral maintenance medication she's taking is working...she has one response, just like the lines from school plays she'd have us rehearse over and over until we knew them like the words to a favorite song: "I'm fine!" Her bright insistence has a way of deflecting my question, but I know her well enough to understand this reaction is not out of avoidance. It's proof of her refusal ever to feel sorry for herself.

When she made the decision to retire, it was because the education environment has changed so much. She says that in more than forty years, she'd never experienced the challenges she's faced in the past few.

"You want to know the real problem in the world today?" she says. "Here's an example: I couldn't get together with you on Friday because they called me to chaperone a field trip with Father Daghir and the kids— what a great young priest. You know him, right? Well, the bishop steps out to take an audience with the students— that's a big deal to you and me, right? Then we went down to tour the cathedral. Here's what I'm finding, Kris: These kids have no focus. No faith. I want to say to them, 'Come on, grab on to something! Believe in something! Show some faith in *something*!' And these are good kids," she says. "They're all good kids. Remember how proud you used to feel just to go to our school? Spirit Week, sports teams—remember the weekends you'd spend working with your classmates on a project? After forty years, they almost ended our mock trial program, until I said I'd come back and lead it." She throws up her hands in exasperation. "These kids are floundering. We want them to be mature and well-adjusted, but nobody knows how to get them there. Meanwhile, the system has gotten frantic to keep kids engaged, and it's very clear to me that we have dumbed down the curriculum. *Citizen Kane* and *Oedipus Rex*—we don't teach those things anymore. They are not teaching *Huck Finn, The Great Gatsby*—"

"They're not teaching *Gatsby*?"

"Nope. All the standards that you were brought up with are gone. Kids can't concentrate, they're multitasking, and everything is a game. Scores were awful, so you know what schools did? They eliminated tests."

She taught the whole person by first *seeing* the whole person, and actively choosing to *love* the whole person. But technology has shaped kids so much today. When I reflect on this in the company of some teacher friends, a theme that emerges is that it seems many teachers these days feel like they don't have parents' blessing to shape children's understanding in the way teachers had been revered for doing for most of modern history. Many teachers feel their hands are tied from advocating for the child's intellectual, emotional, social, and, in some cases, spiritual growth. Between the societal shifts—issues like social media, bullying, and school violence—and a changed family system helmed by parents who have a lot on their plates and meanwhile have their own strong beliefs, I gather that teachers have also never felt a greater need to make sacrifices for their students. Exploring my journey with my great teacher becomes an opportunity to share what steadfast love ends up meaning for a child's future.

For every Mrs. Korthaus—for every favorite teacher any one of us still treasures—teaching isn't a job. It's a living profession. Mrs. Korthaus had a way of getting through to us because she was teaching from the perspective of a grown-up who'd intentionally put herself in situations that either thrilled her or challenged her, but in both cases made her wiser, made her stronger, and made her richer in life experience. What lives on with the student is not what the teacher teaches, but who the teacher is. A kid perceives that the way a teacher teaches inside the class is the way they live outside. A powerful educator not only helps a subject make sense but also, in their own special way, helps life make more sense.

I once ghostwrote a book for a billionaire philanthropist who told me the most generous gift one human can ever give another is their time, because time is the one commodity we can never earn back. Mrs. Korthaus gave us forty years. I recognize there are thousands of teachers out there who are just as committed to their students as she's been. In a time that's arguably harder for educators than ever before, I like to think we all have a Mrs. Korthaus...that instructor who makes it tough to imagine the path we might have taken if they hadn't been called, and so committed, to education. When we're sitting in someone's classroom, we usually have no idea that for the decades to come we'll end up cherishing this person and the sheer amount of themselves they shared with us.

Our project is quickly teaching me that they usually don't, either.

I push as much as I can. I encourage them, get them connected with people who can give them advice or share their own "success story." Our area has a large amount of generational poverty, and the only way these kids will ever break it is if they have someone pushing them and fighting for them. Success can be scary, and when you don't have examples of it around you, it becomes unimaginable.

—Mrs. Sayers, district director of interventions, former elementary principal (and my fourth-grade teacher in 1989–90)

CHAPTER TWO

THE VEHICLE

As NATURALLY AS SHE CONNECTED WITH US, IT'S intriguing that initially Mrs. Korthaus's training as an educator was almost nonexistent. When she was fresh out of college, a priest friend offered her a job teaching social studies at a Catholic school.

"I hadn't taken social studies since eighth grade," she says, cracking open the oven door to peek at a small roast she has for us inside. "But I began staying one lesson ahead of the students. That worked for a while, until I partied too late one night and didn't read up on the duel between Alexander Hamilton and Aaron Burr. So in class, I pulled the classic 'Look it up and come back with the answer tomorrow'—which I had to do, too."

"*That's* why teachers do that?"

"Ha!" She walks over to slide a small cheese board my way across her kitchen island. "I quickly realized that what I loved about *teaching* was *learning*. Teaching was the best way to share that, so I started taking classes to get my certification."

But then came Sister McArdle, the principal of the high school. "Oh, she was quite impressed with herself," she says in a low growl. "When she walked in the room, everyone was to rise—but when she walked into my classroom, well, I would not stand up." She shrugs. "I was called into her office, and…let's just say that a couple years into my short teaching career, it became apparent that I should start making arrangements to secure alternative employment, if you get my drift."

I find myself needing to unstick my chin from the palm of my hand. In our school, rising from our chairs in unison to greet any religious person or school administrator when they entered the classroom was as routine as saying our morning prayers and the Pledge of Allegiance. The teacher typically cues the class with their own example in this act of reverent obedience. To hear of her defiance is enamoring. She is *never* fake. It's sensational.

At the time Mrs. Korthaus was hired, the principal of our Catholic high school was a woman, a wife and a mom, in a time when the school had previously only been led by male priests and the leader of nearly every other organization back home was a man.

"The local Catholic school always had a job open," she says. "I put my résumé in to sub, met with the principal, and found that I had much in common with her thinking. I believed in the philosophy of the school: to teach the whole person."

It was unusual for most of us to encounter a woman carrying herself with such unbridled exuberance who talked about a life path that wasn't cookie-cutter conventional. She held space for that conversation, not in a strong-armed or offensive way, but in a way that for decades made us want to gather around the glow of her self-assurance and wisdom, like a nighttime fire ring after a day out with the ski club she sometimes chaperoned.

It's that authenticity that decades later would help produce a new generation of rural girls. There were the education majors she'd go on to inspire, a few who'd then wind up leading classrooms just down the hall from hers. There were the social workers and healthcare professionals, business leaders and entrepreneurs. One student was a grade behind me and went on to play basketball at Duke and then as a pro in Europe. One a few years ahead of me became an FBI agent in Washington, DC. Then there was the one who had every intention of pleasing her dad by becoming a doctor, like him, before she entered medical school only to realize she wanted to study English...in England.

"She's much younger, but you know her, right?" Mrs. Korthaus asks me. "She's getting her master's in the classics at Oxford!"

One of my old friends had been as determined as I was

to marry a hometown boy before she went on to have a career as a senior global director for some of the biggest beauty brands in the world, including more than a decade with Chanel.

For whichever class of students she was teaching in a given year, the classroom was Mrs. Korthaus's platform for being the hype girl for students who'd graduated. "This weekend I was at the wedding of a past student in *Pittsburgh*," she'd share with fanfare, knowing that to our ears this sounded very cosmopolitan. "I happened to run into a former student who recently finished law school and is now working for *the state attorney general's office*. She has set quite a path for herself, wouldn't you say?"

This was one of her ways of making exciting goals feel within reach for a bunch of small-town kids. We were being invited to realize that we even had dreams.

Still, that brief start as a teacher had made her a fish out of water, and it was those situations, when she found herself the outsider, that came to define her ability to quickly adapt—a fish *to* water, in the end. Mrs. Korthaus tells me how, in her upbringing, she often felt she was being tugged in two opposite directions: between the old ways for women to live their lives, and a new way she'd never even witnessed yet. That's also exactly how a lot of us girls felt during the four years we were in her classroom: We didn't want to go backward, but we were unsure about what lay ahead.

Her parents had settled in a small riverside borough forty miles from Pittsburgh that counted manufacturing among its biggest industries and Catholics its largest population. Her hometown and mine were ninety minutes apart and, from the sound of it, culturally identical. "As much as my Italian family was trying to integrate into the mosaic of American life, they still maintained the past system," she says. "My grandmas cooked and cleaned. I grew up in a family where my mother's beauty shop cash register was pretty much how we lived." Her father, she tells me for the first time, professed to have a career as a "manufacturer's rep."

"We were never sure what he did," she says. "We think he was in the mafia." What he was for sure, she shares, was a drinker. So was her mom. "Fighting, drinking," Mrs. Korthaus says. "My mother slaved over her beauty shop, at the loss of her children because she had to be in that shop working and providing."

Because several of her relatives had moved from Italy to Pennsylvania with the original goal of finding work in the coal mines together, when she needed a break from the tension at home, she could go to play at her cousins' houses. Where we're from, faith was the center of the family, so one of her first experiences on her own was at a camp started by a priest who wanted to get city kids out into nature. "It was at Camp Rosary that I met Sis McSwigan, the camp counselor who taught me to swim and became an important influence in my life."

A few years later, Sis married one of the brothers who owned Seven Springs, the popular Pennsylvania ski and golf resort. The couple started having kids and knew just who to ask when they needed a personal assistant to their family, a plucky, hardworking teenager who'd breezily keep their littles busy. "Every summer, holiday, and most weekends, I would go to Seven Springs to do anything they needed me to do," she tells me. "I was nanny and lifeguard to the kids, I waited tables, worked in the ski shop, and became the activities director." In total, Sis gave birth to nine daughters that Mrs. Korthaus cared for, including teaching them how to swim, just as Sis had taught her.

In our English classes, Mrs. Korthaus taught us about the technique of using a "vehicle" in a story: an object or character that shows up at different points throughout the narrative to symbolize the progress that's being made toward the protagonist's goal or objective (or, at times, the lack of progress). We'd earned extra credit for going to see *Schindler's List* at the movies. Later in class, she asked us whether we remembered the little girl in the red coat against the rest of the black-and-white scenery.

It was impossible to forget her. The first image of that playful child conveyed purity and innocence. As the story continued and we later saw her body being carried away among a pile of others, it communicated the heartless brutality of the Holocaust. "That was a vehicle," Mrs. Korthaus explained. It helped us emotionally and intellectually connect the dots between critical points of the story. *Wow. Look how much has happened.*

In a way, her learning to swim became a literal vehicle for her life. "As the resort grew, I got to grow with it. The family was able to count on me, and they made me a part of everything they were doing. I was skiing in Vail. I traveled with them to the islands as their nanny."

"That was a ticket for you, huh?"

She closes her fist, as if in victory. "It was *the* ticket."

LEARNING TO SWIM WAS SYMBOLIC OF THE EARLY MOTIL-ity in her life, a reason and a means to get away from home when her family environment wasn't pleasant. I've always admired how Mrs. Korthaus spends her spare time: playing tennis and golf or skiing. They're sports you can learn young and practice for a lifetime, either just for fun or to enrich life socially and professionally. When she retired from emceeing our annual high school auction, I bought the prized possession she'd donated to the fundraiser: her personal set of women's golf clubs. The men in my family have always been the golfers. My grandma learned the sport to spend time with my grandpa and couples they knew through business. Mrs. Korthaus learned it for herself—never to be left out of the fun or business conversations.

Sports had been intimidating for me—they were for the boys. Back in third grade, when my younger brother and our cousin, who was my brother's best friend, joined the swim team, my mom encouraged me to try it too. I remember my first swim meet, reaching the wall and yanking off my goggles to realize I'd won third place. Swimming, I saw, was the perfect sport for me: If I didn't have to chase or steal a ball from someone else, if I was just competing against myself, then all I had to do to win was keep swimming faster. By the end of the season, I'd earned a record number of blue ribbons, and my coach said she couldn't wait to get me back in the pool the following year. "I see big things for this kid," she told my mom.

But I never went back. That following year, I turned ten and decided I didn't want the people in the stands or the teammate I had a crush on to see me in a swimsuit. It would take another four years, until junior high, to meet Mrs. Korthaus, who'd diffuse my insecurities. She'd teach me that developing a talent was a far more important point than what you looked like when you were pursuing it.

Over the years, she worked with me on my insecurities so I could start to understand my own objective clearly: to individuate and be my own person with confidence.

During one of our writing sessions, she lets me in on why she so intimately understood what I'd felt so often as the lone girl among males in my family. "To be the first-born daughter meant that we had to be just like the boys, but better," Mrs. Korthaus reflects. I know just what she means: to be the best, to be confident and highly intelligent, but with the added expectations that we'll also be beautiful, forever sweet while never controversial, always at the ready to take care of others in the family, and delighted to tend to the chores around the house while the males invest their time in endeavors that earn them either money to provide for the family or power within the community—usually both at the same time. Mrs. Korthaus's objective wasn't to be pleasing enough to men to one day win the job of taking care of one.

Every time I watch a swimming event during the Olympics, I wonder: *How far could I have gone?* I can imagine that as a kid, Mrs. Korthaus was so determined to adapt—just as Charles Darwin said was necessary to survive, as we learned in Mrs. Chollock's biology class—that she would have barreled right through any worry about what somebody thought of her appearance. As girls, if we can push ourselves past that fear, it opens up a lot of life for us.

I want the girls I teach to be self-confident and not make themselves smaller or less-than in a way previous generations of women were taught to. I want them to value themselves and see their worth. And I know this sounds old-fashioned, but I want them to value and protect their bodies.

—Miss Duplessis, New York City middle school special education teacher

CHAPTER THREE

LIBERAL ARTS

IN MY LATE GRADE SCHOOL YEARS, THE BOYS IN MY FAM-
ily stuck with sports, traveling from one practice to the
next and one season to the next, with no baggage except
the duffel bag they carried. These activities made them
stronger, more social, grew their confidence and prepared
them for the day they'd take over the family manufacturing business. I'd fully departed from swimming and
instead taken to theater, where in Catholic grade school
the costumes—a lamb at the Nativity; Mary, the mother
of Jesus—were forgivingly bulky and hid my shape. As
females in the nineties, we knew what we *weren't* supposed

to be—fat, essentially—but that didn't give us a whole lot of direction about what we *were* supposed to be.

One afternoon in eighth-grade math class, panic suddenly consumed me. Only later was I able to identify the source of that anxiety: overwhelm about the future. The ever more complex algebra formulas on the board in front of me were a microcosm, another word from English class, which symbolized all the uncertainty that lay ahead. My choices were: (A) find a man who'd make decisions for my life, or (B) figure life out for myself, from scratch. In that case, I'd have to learn how to make a living like my dad did, how to fight on the phone when the utilities company overcharged you for a bill, how to buy a house. My parents used to tell the story of how when they first got married, my mom started crying after a call with their landlord. After, she asked my dad to take care of all their finances for the rest of their married life. The unknowns sounded terrifying, and *most* impossible to understand was my middle school dilemma: (A) How do I get a guy to like me, especially if I give off vibes that I don't need him? Or (B) was I being so needy that I made boys run the other way?

I watched *Oprah* after school and searched the pages of *Seventeen*, but nobody seemed to have a clear answer. I wanted to have a family, but I wanted to *be* my own person too. I wanted to have love in my life, but I also wanted to have a mission in life.

This is gonna be really hard, I thought. But I was determined to find my way.

I still had yet to encounter the phenomenon the older

kids called "Mrs. Korthaus," but early that winter, she held auditions for the school's first-ever spring play, which was said to be an ambitious one: the spiritual musical *Godspell.* Our school didn't even have a proper space to produce a musical; our makeshift auditorium was the gymnasium where the cigarette-scented tarps usually used for the Thursday-night church bingo ladies were laid down to protect the wood floor from chairs and the audience's high heels. If you weren't keen to carry your own folding chair onto the floor to see the show, no problem— we hometown basketball fans had developed a tolerance for the agony of sitting on the solid wood bleachers put there in the 1960s. The acoustics? Terrible.

But from the way the older kids talked about Mrs. Korthaus, it was clear she was unstoppable. I hadn't been planning to try out, but a few of my teachers twisted my arm and talked me into it. I was one of the youngest to audition. At tryouts, Mrs. Korthaus announced that the whole cast were the principals—there were no small parts. I was relieved this meant there was zero chance they'd cast me. "Father Walk *loves Godspell*," Mrs. Korthaus said. Father Walk was the new junior–senior high school headmaster, very cultured and intimidatingly stoic. "I'm becoming a producer so he can be the director."

A producer? A director? This sounded serious. Why was I even here? I was out of my league.

But shortly after the end of Christmas break, the echo of Father Walk's measured, steady voice came over the school's PA system. We were at the point of no return: They were about to announce the cast.

"Will the following students please meet in the music room after dismissal." With Father Walk, this wasn't a question. It was an expectation.

When he read out my name, I walked alone to the music room, where I found three seniors, a couple juniors, one freshman, one sophomore, and one friend from my class whose older brother had also been cast. Mrs. Korthaus enthusiastically greeted us and began to tell us our parts.

"You're the vamp!" she told me.

My first thought was: *She seems to recognize me.* It seemed as though she already knew me.

My next thought was: *The vamp?*

I was still hesitant about wearing anything that showed my skin before a sea of eyes. Right away my mom and I found a long-sleeved leotard and leggings that left plenty to the imagination. To complete the look, Mrs. Korthaus hung a pink feather boa around my neck and gave me a pair of flat ballet slides. "I'll get my own but will need to wear these for a couple rehearsals," I said.

"Don't worry about it!" she said and waved me off. "They're yours now."

She'd just met me, and she was fully intent on giving me something that belonged to her. In time, I would come to see that's simply who she is.

She lived in the neighborhood where my family had just moved a mile up the road, but I only vaguely knew her through church. Now that I had a part in the play, she'd start driving me to play practice every evening. I remember wondering how we'd fill the space of the fifteen-minute car ride to school, but immediately she was the easiest grown-up, besides my parents, that I'd ever carried on a conversation with. With Mrs. Korthaus, there was not even a breath's worth of awkwardness. It felt exclusive, in a way, to be the one showing up with her every night.

The night that rehearsals started, the silence among us made it clear that I wasn't the only one who felt daunted by the challenge of this musical. "The play premiered in the early 1970s," Mrs. Korthaus explained. "That was at Carnegie Mellon University—close to home, right?—then moved to New York to be produced off-Broadway. The characters are non-biblical representations of figures who are, in fact, known to appear in Matthew's account of the Gospel. It's been called controversial," she said, hanging on to the letter *l* in the word. "This is a non-traditional take on Christianity that focuses less on dogma"—which somehow managed to gain a third syllable—"and *more* on the universality of Jesus's love. Some might call it 'liberal.' I call it liberal arts. Some of you know what I say in class: If you've been educated with a liberal arts foundation, you can do anything in the world."

She then got down to work, filling us in on our parts in the production. "In *Godspell*, if one of you is onstage, you're all onstage. Except for one intermission, it's all of you, right out here." She gestured grandly before her from the center of our gymnasium stage.

There was a palpable dumbfoundedness among us. No break from character? No costume changes? No two minutes to race backstage, sweating, and use the bathroom?

"So you have to be a very, very homogenous group of

singers and actors—and every single one of you gets your own song as a solo. For now, Jacob will join you on piano, and that will be the only accompaniment until we make it to dress rehearsals. Then we're bringing in professional musicians."

Jacob, my shy but wickedly talented classmate, was clearly trying to hide that he felt as daunted as the rest of us, but for this play and in the years to come, Mrs. Korthaus's reliance on his piano playing would draw him out of his shell.

"The set," she said, "is just as stripped down as the music. Our only backdrop will be scaffolding." We understood that without an elaborate, colorful set like the ones our moms had volunteered to decorate in grade school, there was nothing to distract or charm the audience if our singing and acting weren't outstanding.

As rehearsals got underway, Father Walk always sat as far away from the stage as he could to get the broadest vantage point on the action, and Mrs. Korthaus was always up close and personal with us. When we would take breaks—which, from the start, we saw would be rare—we'd see the two of them joining up to quietly discuss where we needed to fine-tune. This whole thing had been Father Walk's brainchild, but he knew Mrs. Korthaus's strengths in connecting with us students and moving an audience. She was fully in the lead.

My character, the vamp, turned out to be pretty G-rated. The role had been originated by Sonia Manzano, the actress who inspired children for over forty years as Maria on *Sesame Street*. On our car rides, Mrs. Korthaus and I talked a lot about my character, who was written to represent the redemption of the prostitute Mary Magdalene and to convey how holy God's view of women is. She invited me to think about how others had judged Mary Magdalene and how Jesus had recognized her struggle, drew her to Him, and made her one of His closest disciples. In the play, she's a redeemed and unapologetic presence who flirts with the audience to get their attention so that ultimately she can preach God's love to them.

During a phase in my life when portraying a confident female took some doing, Mrs. Korthaus gave me the floor so I could witness and grow my own talent—my *own* promise as a woman, my power to spread God's goodness. She showed me I had options, different ways of being in the world. The play itself showed us that the narrow understanding we had of a God of obedience and expectation could just as logically be of a God who is all-loving, all-embracing, and all-inclusive. We also learned the word *Catholic* means universal. Jesus welcomed, accepted, and loved everyone. This perspective on His humanity deepened the faith of this motley band of budding theater kids, inspiring us to work together and give the show—and Him—our all.

I was performing almost entirely with upperclassmen, and we took on Mrs. Korthaus's challenge to become a cohesive unit that would complement one another. In the cast were three male athletes, a few church kids, the choreographer for the cheerleading squad, two senior girls who had to adjust their part-time job schedules around rehearsals, and a couple of kids who weren't involved in any other activities at all. As rehearsals went on, the differences between us no longer mattered. In her lovingly no-nonsense way, Mrs. Korthaus made it clear from the first rehearsal that we were all stakeholders in the show's success. From that point, our cooperation as a group was settled. We ate meals together. During study halls, some of us got together to run lines. We became close and supported each other's success. I wasn't playing sports, but I was part of a team.

And we needed to be: Mrs. Korthaus was a one-woman PR mastermind. She'd landed us a feature in the weekend newspaper and set up an interview with the full cast on a local radio show, both of which meant we got to leave school and travel to the interviews together. It was the first time anyone besides the athletes had received special privileges. Her critics in the community had predicted that *Godspell* would be too complicated to pull off, too radical to support, and too irrelevant to care about. She never listened. Instead, she appeared increasingly effortless in proving them wrong. The buzz was building. This show was becoming a machine.

My solo would end intermission, so my presence had to be fiercely commanding. I couldn't be shy about capturing the audience's attention and making it clear the show was starting again. To make it even more dynamic, Mrs. Korthaus and Father Walk decided I should make my entrance from the back of the audience. The lights would go down, the spotlight would turn on, and I'd step into the beam as the final cue that the crowd should quiet down. Then I'd walk down the middle aisle, pretending to be a heartbreaker.

Night after night, I was nervous before my performance, but as I made my way to the stage, the rest of the cast would be waiting to enfold me into the ensemble. There were no more labels: Backstage, one of the older boys in the cast zipped up my leotard in the most protectively platonic way, and when the intermission lights dimmed to signal me to hit my pose, a castmate accepted the half-chewed piece of gum I'd been using to keep my throat from drying out.

My stomach was in knots whenever I had to perform my number, but at our first dress rehearsal a week before opening night, there was no turning back. "Gimme shimmy!" Mrs. Korthaus called out from the back of the gym—hilarious direction for a bunch of Catholic school students. "Work it!"

"Working it" took some work for this kid. Any degree of self-possession I had was being cultivated, rehearsal by rehearsal. Because Mrs. Korthaus believed in my confidence, by the time dress rehearsals arrived, I stepped onto that stage in all-black spandex and black ballet shoes, still wrapped in the hot pink feather boa that smelled like a cooler that hadn't been opened since last summer. At the start of the show, I always sought out a familiar face whom I could tease during my number—usually my two grandfathers and Mrs. Korthaus's husband, who turned endearingly red even in the dark.

As a cast we had *synergy*, as Mrs. Korthaus put it. It was the chemistry among everyone who'd touched it that made it a success, all trickling down from the vision of one woman. With her leading us, we created something our town hadn't experienced before.

She taught me that whatever I'm feeling when I'm writing or performing is exactly how the audience is going to feel when they take in the work. "Do you believe it?" she'd shout. "Make *them* believe it!" For the first time, I believed it.

Under her leadership, our arts program became a powerful force—a vehicle—in moving perceptions forward in my hometown. With a professional band and sold-out crowds that demanded we revive the production that following summer, this time inside the community theater, she showed all of us. Our "Jesus" would be accepted into one of the toughest theater programs in the country. Our "Judas" went on to act in Hollywood. Even the proudest jocks started auditioning, sometimes singing and dancing, and competing for deeply expressive roles.

Mrs. Korthaus was among the first—possibly *the* first—to urge me to step into my power, to experience the glory of making a commitment and sticking with it. I saw that I could stand alone and face a crowd, not run away, and that there was a world beyond what was typical for our hometown—that there were possibilities that weren't so threatening for a girl. I still didn't know what I wanted in life, but for the first time, I believed I'd find it. By taking on this production, she was thinking bigger for us than we'd have ever dared to. I think we all felt that way.

With the response the show received, that aching young teen in me realized I'd been included in, had even contributed to, something that had led some people in our community to feel changed, to see art and expression and maybe even their faith, a little differently.

Back in her kitchen, we're talking about it. "A lot for you started with *Godspell*," she says. "That was a defining moment in your life." Suddenly she's distracted by the bite of sautéed vegetables she's testing from her wooden spoon.

I'm struck by how practiced she is at having a big discussion about life while moving through a practical, everyday act like making a meal. That's her: equal parts provocative and nurturing. "Mmm!" she cries. "Wait 'til you try this old dish from my family: greens and beans."

After *Godspell*, I worked with her on almost a dozen more plays and continued with theater in college before I got paid to appear in a couple of shows. She'd become that producer, that woman whose leadership, creativity, and connections had wrangled moving parts to bring something to life that had just months prior only been an idea. She'd managed deadline pressure and coached us to hit every step, every note, every line in a two-and-a-half-hour musical that took a level of determination and stamina that only certain instructors can inspire.

So the first time I met Mrs. Korthaus, it actually wasn't in her classroom or our neighborhood. There's that saying, *When the student is ready, the teacher appears*. It was as though she swung into my life from stage left at the moment I was realizing that I needed "to see it to be it."

Our role is to model and advocate for acceptance. Gandhi said, "No one is born hating another. If you can be taught to hate, you can be taught to love; for love is more natural of the two." It's my go-to philosophy: Our role is to teach students to love themselves and to love others.

—Mrs. Benton, school district superintendent in rural Pennsylvania

CHAPTER FOUR

HUMANITIES

WHEN THEY WERE LITTLE, CAROL AND HER YOUNGER sisters would earn a few coins for sweeping up hair from the floor of their mom's beauty parlor, lingering to eavesdrop as the old ladies filled the salon with gossip and tales. It makes sense that this was the foundation for the life of a girl drawn to storytelling and language— not to mention the self-assurance, the "aplomb," as she'd say, inside women when our guards are down, when the purple toner's setting or the plastic perm rods are in and we're left to be ourselves, sharing our hearts with one another.

We're back at the country club when I learn why she first fell in love with the humanities, the arts, and liberal arts: She intentionally gripped any chance to surpass the circumstances she'd been born into. "When I had an opportunity, I'd find any way to get out of the atmosphere I was in," she says. "I started to do things that would distinguish me from the crowd."

"Like what?"

"Well, let's see. Like winning a history medal in eighth grade, and excelling in forensics. I was among the top point-scorers in extemporaneous speakers. I had leads in all the musicals, and I couldn't even sing that well. I was *that* motivated to make my life better: I used every vehicle to get out—and I did."

I had leads in all the musicals, and I couldn't even sing that well. Her quintessential guts. "That's the humanities and liberal arts foundation: being able to adapt, not to be intimidated," she says.

Her path to creating her vision of education and teaching started when she entered Catholic school. At the end of eighth grade, her father told her she'd be going to an all-girls school, leaving behind her friends and their excitement to join the cheerleading squad together in the fall. "Dad always said that he didn't have money to give us, but he would see that we had a good education," she says. "What he meant was that I would be with 'better people' who could become a network for me to grow." She hated the Catholic school for the first two weeks...until the most popular and beautiful senior in the school took her under her wing.

"I had been chosen!" Mrs. Korthaus says. Then her school experience picked up momentum. "I ran for class office, got accolades for public speaking. I even had a boyfriend whose dad was the president of one of the biggest manufacturers in the region," she continues. "I learned from him how to eat using proper utensils, not to place milk cartons on the table—rules not commonly followed at the table in my home. It was a stretch keeping up, but somehow I always managed."

She says many parents sent their daughters to college "to find the perfect mate." She had followed that boyfriend, George, from Pennsylvania to Washington, DC, because George was at Georgetown. "Yep," she says, noting my amusement. "His name was George, and he went to Georgetown. I was at Dunbarton College of Holy Cross while he was studying international law, but he was a drinker. Right after we got to DC, we were tailgating at a polo match on the bank of the Potomac—now, what kind of hotshot do you think you've become when you're tailgating at polo matches? Well, that's what we did. Until George got drunk, picked up an anchor off the riverbank, and swung it so hard that he literally drove it right up his ass."

Her eyes flash with pleasure when I can't control my laughter. "He ended up going home, buying a bar, and dying very young of alcoholism. After he left college, I never saw him again." She smooths the country club table linen in front of her, as if she wishes she could have made George's end less messy. "That's what happens when you follow a boy because you think that's what you're supposed to do."

She stayed in DC and focused instead on her academics. "My college was one of the most prestigious institutions of higher learning. In fact, Howard University's law school operates on our old campus. I'd earned a scholarship there, and I was mortified: Did the other girls know how poor I was? Well, they found out on move-in day at the dorms."

Her parents wanted her to marry a Georgetown lawyer or doctor, or a midshipman from the Naval Academy. "That was not my goal," she says. "I decided my goal was that I would succeed at learning to navigate this kind of a social milieu. My best friend was from Peru, and I thought, *Well, isn't that cool?* Turned out her dad was the attaché to the Peruvian vice president. She taught me to play bridge. I became freshman class president. I attended the socials at Georgetown and the Naval Academy. I was *accepted* because I was smart—but I *thrived* because I learned how to grow and adapt."

It so happens this was all between 1959 and 1963 when "all hell was breaking loose," she says. "Every Saturday, we caught the bus and rode it up to Baltimore. Dr. King had told us to walk into restaurants and sit in the colored section—"

"Dr. King?"

"I never told you I'd marched with Martin Luther King?" She looks at me in surprise, as if now she intends to fill me in on everything. "'Just be dead weight,' he said. It was the idea of passive resistance, you see. The restaurant staff would have to lift us right out of our chairs, drag us out, and push us back onto the bus. Then the bus would start up again, and we'd go to the next restaurant and do the same thing."

Thinking of a stranger carrying this pocket-sized soul out of a restaurant makes me want to giggle—but then it hits me: what a vulnerable choice that would have been for a young woman, especially one so petite. Not once does she mention any concern for herself. It was the era for pushing forward for progress in the world, she says, and it was just thrilling to participate.

"I remember we escorted the boys from the Naval Academy to John F. Kennedy's inauguration ball on what was, at that time, the snowiest day in Washington, DC's history."

"You went to *JFK's inauguration ball*?"

"I never told you that either?"

She hadn't just read about it in the newspapers or watched it on the TV in her dorm's lounge. She had participated and would later show others—including her students—how to become a part of history. She taught us that we can make a difference by getting up and dancing when it would be safer, easier, more comfortable to sit it out.

With pride, she says, "There was a lot of very, very good effort being made to try to change the thinking," then adds, "And don't forget, that was also during Vatican II!" Older Catholics often talk about this period. We studied it in high school theology, the drastic changes that broke away from some of the most traditional, solemn, and, safe to say, outdated practices in the Catholic

Church. "A lot of everybody's life was being shaken up. When that happened, people's minds began to grow. We had no idea what we were doing, but we knew it was the right thing to do."

In those early days of her teaching career in the sixties, she must have been an amazing social studies teacher. She was an example of civic engagement and of how the world could change with more women out there *in* the world.

I'm reminded that years ago, she sparked my interest in etymology, the study of the origin of words. *Liberty* and *liberal*; the Italian and Spanish *libro* for "book." The word *library*. Does the root *lib* signify "freedom"? Because—isn't that what books, and the arts, and learning are? When I dig deeper, I find that one Latin word for "offspring" is *liber*—which we might take to understand that the word *child* means "free one."

I tell her: "Maybe that's why Jesus told all of us to keep the heart of a child: so that we're free to imagine, and dream, and hope—"

"And learn."

It's too late to call her when I'm pulled out of the bathroom from brushing my teeth before bed by the BBC world news' late-night segment on Afghanistan, months after the United States' departure and the Taliban has taken over. Suicide and self-harm rates among young Afghani women have skyrocketed, they report, because they can't go to school anymore.

I keep listening as I walk back into my bathroom and

stare in the mirror. It feels good to appreciate my education, but tears are dripping from my jaw when I hear of girls who can't experience it. It's not unlike the student who comes to school hungry or in clothes that show struggles at home: The only thing that assures any of us a hopeful future is the pure luck of the place and people we're born to.

I crawl into bed, and I think about the bed I'm lying in. The room around me. The house the room fits in. The property the house sits on...and the sequence of opportunities I've had, just to be able to own this one tiny part of the planet. I think about Mrs. Korthaus who I can be sure is also in bed just around the corner. If a woman has her own home, she doesn't need much else in life. But there's usually a lot of work that goes into having the ability to get there.

We can't take education for granted, though I remember the moments I've resisted giving it my strongest effort. There's only ever been one time I can think of when Mrs. Korthaus got angry with me. In the spring of my senior year, she'd again cast me as one of the principal characters in the annual musical. I was ready for high school to be over while simultaneously fearing all the unknowns I'd face in college—the teachers and some students used to call it "senioritis" when a senior was checked-out and showing angst. I'd been fighting bronchitis through most of rehearsals, and this was the first show I'd been part of where the cast wasn't getting along. As one of the leads, I knew I wasn't doing a very good job actually leading.

The morning of opening night, I decided to take what we'd now call a mental health day because I'd had enough. After taking part in every theatrical production the school had put on since I'd been in eighth grade, I didn't want to do the show.

Later that morning, Mrs. Korthaus walked out on her classes and showed up on my family's front porch. "You need to go out there," my mom said. Ashamed, I stepped outside in my bathrobe.

"You *DO NOT QUIT*, do you hear me?" Mrs. Korthaus said. "What*ever* is going on with you, this show is the finale to your high school theater career."

I cringed at the word. *Career.*

She went on. "I don't give a rat's *ass* about the fact that we're sold out tonight—*which* we are—or that you're going to let an entire town down if you don't go out there. But *YOU* earned this part, and *YOU* owe it to yourself to get out there tonight. So are you gonna show up? Or are you backing out?" She startled me when she continued: "Because if there's even a *chance* you're performing, you have to get to school immediately. You know the rule: no extracurricular events if you're out for more than half the day."

I quietly closed the front door as she cruised out of our driveway to take the shortcut back to school. I put on my uniform slacks and blazer, drove to school, and went onstage that night.

My high school theater career. There she'd stood, cloaking the term around my shoulders as if it were a theater costume…and it struck me: For the first time, the concept didn't feel too big. I looked up the root of the word and found it was related to a carriage, a car, coming from the Latin *carrere*: to journey.

She believed I'd come to see that education is a gift, and the ability to become all we can be in the world is not a chance that everyone gets. And it's usually teachers, especially the ones who put in the extra time—to coach, to direct, to mentor, to advise—who give kids the greatest chance to stretch to their higher potential. Learning, growing, and then building a career—that journey is the freedom to be a lifelong learner. Back then, she was furious that I was being given every opportunity and would dare to squander my chance.

"I SUBBED THE OTHER DAY," SHE TELLS ME OVER DINNER one night. "With all this rain lately the kids can't practice any spring sports. But you know what was interesting?"

"What?"

"The seventh and eighth graders are reading *The Book Thief*, which is based in Nazi Germany. That got me thinking: How about some of the things they're trying to do by banning books? Did I ever tell you how when I was in college in DC marching with Martin Luther King, we also hung Senator Joe McCarthy in effigy?"

My expression in response is proof that I didn't listen to my history teachers as well as I listened to her. "I feel like I should know about this…"

"Look it up," she says.

Smartphones didn't exist in the days I was in her classroom.

Effigy: A roughly made model of a particular person, made in order to be damaged or destroyed as a protest or expression of anger.

By now, she's on a roll. "Banning books? That's McCarthyism! You've heard me talk about this: *The Book Thief* isn't even about Nazi Germany, just like *Huck Finn* is not even about the Civil War."

She's right. In books and movies, we call these events the backdrop the story is set against. The backdrop is a historical context that helps couch the narrator's or protagonist's conflict and helps the audience understand why the stakes in the story are so high. And, as a secondary benefit, it does help to teach history.

"I mean, books are a vehicle to understand history, psychology, philosophy, even religion," she cries. "Those people who get all bent out of shape about books—what would they rather kids focus on, football? They don't realize that sports management and sports psychology lend themselves to these exact kinds of conversations. Even to become a doctor, why, just look at da Vinci: How can you possibly study anatomy and not be fascinated by the work by some of the artists who were also doctors and philosophers? It all works together—as it *should*. Which is what lifelong learning is all about. You cannot begin to talk about any current situation without knowing this kind of background. That comes from studying art and literature. I want students to have access to anything they want to read that helps them see the world and themselves differently."

She doesn't have to school me in this. The most powerful lessons we learn, aside from our own limited experiences, are through other people's stories. A good story, I always say, can change minds, lives, and the world.

I encourage them to think outside the box, and some-times to do this, it helps to take students out of the world that they know. A little spark can start a fire for something they never might have thought of.

—Mrs. Aravich, retired kindergarten teacher

CHAPTER FIVE

TOPICAL

W E ADORED HER, BUT NOT BECAUSE SHE MADE WORK easy. Mrs. Korthaus gave us class assignments that, as demanding as they were, were preparing us for what was coming next in life. She stretched us.

"Let's talk about *term papers*," she'd say in her grand way. "They're due next month; have you been thinking about that? You'll turn in a minimum of eight pages."

"*Eight pages?*" a corner of the room would inevitably respond.

"Double-spaced," she'd retort. "Relax, we're still talking about a month away. But don't"—she'd spin on her heel to face us with her index finger in the air—"I repeat, *don't* wait until the last minute."

"Wrote the whole thing last night," I told her out of the side of my mouth as I piled it onto the stack on her desk.

"Last night! Well." She pretended to recompose herself. "Let's see how that turns out for you."

On the days she handed back our grades, she'd walk around the room in a way that was its own event. While we waited with anticipation, she'd adjust her glasses just-right on the end of her nose, look at each student's name, and place the papers face down on each of our desks. I'd turn over my paper *ever*...so...slowly to read her red ink, convinced that, at some point, her faith in me was sure to expire. But I always let out an exhale to discover the grades—98%, 99%.

After I'd openly confessed that I'd written my paper at the last minute, I stared at my paper, astonished. Assured. As loving as she was, she had high standards, she expected strong work, and she called it out when we delivered anything less. A good grade meant she really believed you were good.

To this day, I don't know how my grades measured up against my classmates'. I was just relieved that even in my least enthusiastic year, I'd mustered enough will to deliver to her expectation. I thought so much of her. Just like the competitive swimming that I'd given up half a decade earlier, this was proof to myself that I had what it took. I had a good coach. She believed I could articulate thoughts well...that I had thoughts worth articulating at all. Her willingness to sit with my writing was an unconditionally accepting outlet. She was my first audience long before I realized a woman, or anyone, could choose writing as a profession.

We looked up to her, in part because she knew what was going on in the world, and *she put us in touch with it*. So we believed her when she said we could make it out there. She was current, she was cool. When most teachers were teaching from the textbooks, Mrs. Korthaus often taught from newspapers and magazines. "This week, the *New York Times* called *Seinfeld* a 'comedy of errors,'" she shared in class one day, wielding a copy of the newspaper in her hand. (It's likely this was the first *New York Times* I'd ever seen in person.) "We've talked about the Greeks and the comedy of errors now, haven't we?"

Nods around the room.

"We often laugh because we relate to the fool and know he'll survive his self-inflicted silliness, while in contrast, the character we admire draws out our tears. We cry for the pain we know and the pain we can't imagine."

She never ceased to impress us with how well she could connect the lesson with the things we actually cared about. Who else could tie together classical Greek theater and Jerry Seinfeld in a lesson? "No soup for *you*!" the boys would shout back and forth in the hallway. She was bringing New York, the cultural center of our times, into a rural Pennsylvania classroom. Shows like *Friends* and *Seinfeld* captured the spirit of the times—"the *Zeitgeist*!" she called it—that we lived in: friendships, including between men and women, that were no longer based on the construct of two genders being obligated to each other's needs. These relationships were life-enriching, with laughter and trust at the center. Mrs. Korthaus was spotlighting these cultural representations that showed us a path into the next phase of our lives that wasn't a direct march toward marriage.

From her I came to understand why so many newspapers are called "the *Times*": because their role in our lives is to equip us with the information of this moment and connect our everyday reality to the era that we live in. Back then I couldn't have known how precious it is to live in a society where journalism is protected so that we citizens know what our leaders are deciding on our behalf— nor could I have known that a lifetime of sitcom reruns would always take me back to structures of thought I'd learned to develop as early as high school. The brilliance in her instruction would be timeless, just like the humor on *Seinfeld*.

She taught us to tune in to the news every day—any source of news. I'd picked up a paper route to earn a little money and read the front page of our local newspaper while I rolled the neighbors' copies into tight cylinders and slipped a rubber band around them, the ink staining my fingertips gray and making them smell like oil. I walked and biked through the Pennsylvania winter to deliver those papers while one of the widows on my route, Mrs. Fisher, would lean out from her kitchen door to holler across the howling wind: "It builds character, honey!" I positioned my head crown-first against the storm and kept moving.

My friend David listened to Mrs. Korthaus, making his

first stock purchase based on a tip she'd given him out of something she'd read in *USA Today*. Only rarely did David talk about how hard it was to be from the only Asian family in our school, but Mrs. Korthaus had a way of fostering a sense of belonging among a class, which helped each of us excel in our own ways. David went on to manage screenwriters at one of the big three Hollywood talent agencies.

Even years later there were certain sections of the news that I felt unqualified to understand, convinced they were over my head. Topics like international relations, politics, and finance all seemed so complex, but as Mrs. Korthaus encouraged us to expose ourselves to subjects like these, she showed us how just having an awareness of these things was a way to be part of what was happening in the world. I'd come to see it wasn't a lot different from following the soap operas my mom usually watched on the kitchen TV—paying a little bit of attention each day could help me catch up.

But there were a couple works she introduced to us that were both topical, which means relevant to our lives in the present day, and evergreen, or enduringly applicable. In advanced English, Mrs. Korthaus pulled out the Greek play *Lysistrata*. "This is far beyond anything most instructors teach in an AP English class at a Catholic school, okay, you guys?" she prefaced. "This is some serious feminist stuff," she said, even as every class in our school marched in the annual pro-life rally through the middle of town. To our ears, the word *feminist* was its own f-bomb.

But she was unswerving, and so were we. Just imagine, she invited us; imagine a world where women knew how powerful they were, that if we really wanted to, we could end wars by making men listen to us by withholding physical intimacy.

Is that it? I wondered. Did world peace come down to access to the female body?

No, we'd discuss. That wasn't the point. The point was, in an evolved society, sex is an exercise that's chosen when both partners trust and respect each other's hearts and minds. The world is at its best when relationships are in harmony, when women feel safe in their lives and have the choice to engage in a partnership that's equitable, loving, and healthy.

Then there was *A Doll's House* by Henrik Ibsen. In 1879, this Norwegian male playwright was saying that, in ways minor and significant, women deserved to have financial independence and unwavering regard inside of marriage. Ibsen's ending of the play was most satisfying: The protagonist, Nora, walks out on a patriarchal husband who'd emotionally tortured her for having an affair that he'd entirely imagined.

I hadn't learned a self-assured response or gotten any fierce-minded guidance about how to respond when a boy wasn't sweet to me. In songs, in the movies, couples usually got back together after a fight; on soap operas, they secretly never got over each other but went on in silent heartbreak to marry other partners. When a guy pushed my buttons, I somehow grew up believing it was my job to simply play the part and react. To have someone angry at me or unwilling to love me unconditionally was destroying. The idea that heartbreak was just as simple a choice as permanently walking away with my chin up had never dawned on me before Mrs. Korthaus introduced us to literature with female characters making brave choices.

I started to seek out more stories focused on women who broke out from the perceived limitations life imposed on them. For a term project, I presented an in-depth analysis of *A Doll's House* to our class while Mrs. Korthaus nodded subtly from the back of the classroom. Nora was an example of how there's often a very fine line between the chance to become the young woman who finds herself trapped in unhappiness in the interest of sticking with the life she knows, and the one who defines her own destiny. As I delivered that presentation, Mrs. Korthaus could see that her influence around women's empowerment was something I was starting to internalize.

Still, I needed to be nudged to start to explore and embody this in real life. When Mrs. Chollock, our biology teacher, had taken such a shine to her French language lessons that she planned the school's first-ever summer trip to Europe, Mrs. Korthaus had to shame us into seeing how lucky we were that our parents could send us. In the planning meeting, Miss Showers was wearing a sombrero, and Mrs. Chollock was wearing a beret. We students were slumped in the desk seats set up in a U shape in Miss Showers's classroom—the languages room.

There were a few of my friends here, mostly older kids I'd had a few classes with, and none of us seemed very excited. Why *Europe*? In eighth grade I'd been pulled out of taking Latin with the rest of my class and instead placed into German—*German*—with the high school kids, which I viewed more as a favor from the school guidance counselor, who was a friend of my parents, than a testament to my language placement scores. This trip to Europe was another example of how my parents would give me the chance to try something I might discover I was passionate about... but I didn't know who that would make me.

The least exciting part was that the July trip to Europe meant we would miss some of the most anticipated moments of the summer—sleepovers with friends, for starters, not to mention the firemen's parade and days at the pool. London? Paris? Spain? The white cliffs of Dover, the Swiss Alps... Who *cared*?

"...And then we get to Monday, July tenth, and you know what that means," Mrs. Chollock sang. "Arrival in Luxembourg!" She appeared to do a Hawaiian hula dance while Miss Showers shook her maracas, and still none of us had any idea what to expect in Luxembourg.

Well... forever in solidarity with the other teachers and school administrators who were most invested in us, later in class Mrs. Korthaus folded her arms and leaned her bottom against the front of her desk. There was subtext in her action—*subtext*, a word she taught us. This was symbolic, and rare: She was creating physical distance between herself and our class.

In silence she studied us for a moment, a group of kids too inexperienced at life to appreciate this opportunity. None of us had ever been outside the country. I shrunk down in my chair, knowing at least some of this was being directed at me.

"I hope that one day every one of you will get to travel the world," she says. "But for those of you who have the chance to go this summer, this experience will change you!"

Did we...*want* to change?

She started pacing the room in existential reflection. Even her way of butting in had a tenderness to it.

"You have to realize that the world that is presented to us here, in this town, has blinders. We can *see*, and we can *know*, what's in front of us—but anytime we try to move the blinders and open up our vision, that's a pretty big stretch for a lot of people you and I know. If you choose to worry about what's going on at home, you'll see it as nothing more than another bus trip, and you might as well stay home. If you allow yourself to be immersed in the history and the culture, this will change your life."

It changed our lives by first piquing our senses. When we arrived, we smelled the fragrances from French perfume factories along the side streets in Paris; we sipped our first sangria on a hotel rooftop in Barcelona; we stood before the *Mona Lisa*, puzzling over what made her coy expression so iconic, until just a few steps away, the Winged Victory of Samothrace seemed to call to me. *I think I love art.*

We spent an afternoon touring the museum that had been made of Dachau, the German concentration camp. Some students couldn't make it all the way through, but a group of us pressed forward to observe the halls that had once led to the gas chambers; the prison uniforms, some of which had fit toddlers, now hung inside glass shadow boxes. I hadn't understood how significant it was that in World War II, my grandpa drove in some of the US tanks carrying soldiers who would liberate the Jewish people still living in those camps. Now I did. I could feel the lives that had been inside these walls, inside these clothes.

It was an *interesting* cultural experience when we and our teacher chaperones were the only fully clothed humans lounging on a French topless beach. "This is all part of the cultural experience," Mrs. Chollock reminded us with a chirp.

It felt awkward at first, considering two of our chaperones were priests, but we observed the grown-ups' perfectly unfazed reactions and considered, this was not obscene. It was just another way of being. We were learning as much about ourselves as we were about the world.

I remember following our female teachers through airports and train stations, starting with JFK in New York. I'd never seen a woman navigate her own way through a major transportation hub. It clocked in my mind as something I could now be certain was possible.

I WAS WALKING DOWN THE STREET TO BABYSIT THE Hopkins kids when Mrs. Korthaus called out from her garage: "Don't you look good!" When she stepped into the driveway to chat, she was tanned and fit, clearly having spent the past few weeks playing golf and tennis. She stuck her hands inside the pockets of her red cotton shorts and rocked back and forth in her Velcro hiking sandals—her trademark summer look.

"Clearly you're all back safe. Good! Good good good. We'll catch up."

Yet again that September, I'd been placed in advanced German class. When Father Swoger called on me, I cleared my throat. As I translated an entire paragraph of German text out loud on the spot, I could feel both his amazement and mine. I'd heard authentic German spoken *in* Germany, for the first time seeing how this language might be useful someday. I'd also stood among art and history and, heck, a nude beach. I had crossed the borders of five European countries onboard a bus.

This was the power of exposure to culture in a young person's life. It's why even a nature walk can awaken a child's mind, because it nurtures a feeling of connection to the world around them. Certainly not every young person gets the chance to explore outside the country, but any teacher who stokes students' curiosity about the world is encouraging them to take a formative step in seeing themselves as part of a broader worldview, outside the confines of their daily lives. In the grand scheme of things, such a small percentage of kids get to experience this, but the teacher who can instill a personal curiosity about what's happening in other places—what people experience, the weather, the food there—is planting a seed that, in many cases, will profoundly shape who they become.

In particular, a young woman who gets to see what's beyond the parameters of her own world—her romantic relationships, her school, her community, her culture—grows more confident in herself and more compassionate toward others. My English teacher knew, my biology teacher knew: When you give a girl just a *taste* of the world, it's the start of her unfolding. She begins to see herself as part of a place much broader and more beautiful, where just *maybe* she can still hold her own and realize she's way bigger than she thought she was. She perceives herself in a more integrated way; she sees that she can find a sense of belonging just about anywhere. Travel increases a girl's curiosity about the latitude for her life. It makes her more sophisticated, it makes her more confident, and it's the very first glimpse that it's possible for her to stand on her own. On their own time, this group of teachers and chaperones had shown us that the sky was literally the limit for a kid who had their passport before their driver's license.

The following summer when my friends and I planned a beach trip six hours away to Ocean City, my friend Christina's dad held a meeting to teach us girls how to read the printout of directions that he'd created for us using MapQuest, which had just recently launched. It made me think of how my grandpa started his business by traveling across the country using a paper map, even under a dome light in the dark. I was aware that I was growing up just as the world was becoming accessible for females to explore on our own.

I was feeling worldlier and more adventurous, but I still wasn't ready to leave home. By the time acceptance letters arrived from the two universities where I applied,

I knew that my mom and dad wanted me to go to the more distant, famously rigorous college where I'd know only two or three friends and where the preppy students I saw on the campus tour looked more like fresh-faced TV news personalities than kids. It was too polished. It wasn't for me.

It was Mrs. Korthaus who would ultimately persuade me. "Some people have a fear of failure. But you? You have a fear of success. Listen to me: You are going to the toughest university that takes you," she said. "You are going to see the world and have a career. Do you know that when I was in college, girls couldn't even *go* to the university that's accepted you?"

Now she was getting through to me.

In talking about her own college years, she'd called it the "social milieu." I'd need to learn how to become part of it. To adapt. "But it'll be hard," I bellyached.

Her response was a pert clip: "You can play their game."

I want all of my students to feel valued and seen, but it is especially important to me that my female students feel seen and empowered. I want them to know that they have power in their words and through their art. I want to open the world to them and allow them to see that they can grow without limits—because who they are and what they say matter.

**—Mrs. Green, high school art
teacher in rural Pennsylvania**

CHAPTER SIX

POINT OF VIEW

I HAD NEEDED TO DEVELOP MRS. KORTHAUS'S SAME kind of gritty willingness to learn the game, but she was right. By the time I moved to New York City after college, I could almost hear what she was telling her classroom about what I'd been up to by now:

In college, she got an internship at the Cleveland Clinic and then worked nights at an Indian restaurant before she got home and washed the smell of spices out of her hair to wake up at four a.m. and intern at the morning desk for one of Cleveland's local news stations. Then she moved to New York to get her master's in communications, where Jacob, our piano player for all the musicals back in those days, was getting his PhD at NYU. Now he's an immunology professor at a major state university, where he leads a lab that helps develop vaccines against novel viruses—who says art and science aren't complementary? Well, Jacob had a friend who helped Krissy get a job spritzing perfume on customers at Bloomingdale's, and lo and behold, she got an internship at the New York Times, *which she'd never even read before she sat in this classroom. You think that's something?*

Listen to this: While she was trying to save money, she butchered her own haircut. So she goes walking into the neighborhood salon for help, and the stylist just happens to have another client who worked in book publishing and helped Krissy get a foot in the door at Simon & Schuster. What's that tell you? That there are no mistakes? Or how about that it pays to get along with people once you get out in the world? You can take the girl out of the small town...

But not the small town out of the girl, the class might oblige her by chanting back.

In my twenties, I'd visit the school and speak to her classes during my holiday breaks. There were, in fact, some storied moments in those early New York years when I was just trying to break into publishing and media. The first time I rode in an elevator with Stephen King, I couldn't get the words out to share that I was writing my graduate thesis about his book *On Writing*. When a celebrity launched a memoir or a children's book, they sometimes came to the office to sign copies for us employees and we'd all line up outside the conference room, chattering with excitement for our turn to meet them. It was serendipitous when the very first celebrity book signing I attended was with Sonia Manzano—who had been one of my earliest teachers as Maria on *Sesame Street*, and who originated the part in *Godspell* that I'd played a decade earlier. "You've got to be kidding," Mrs. Korthaus said.

I've heard these referred to as "God winks": the undeniable signs that God was completing promises that string the events of life together to make them all make sense. This, I was starting to see, was what Mrs. Korthaus had meant—she wanted me to go experience all the miracles that were out there for me. At a rooftop party looking out across the New York skyline, stepping off the subway to arrive right on the edge of Central Park, when on my lunch breaks I could walk one block east to St. Patrick's Cathedral on Fifth Avenue, which I'd first visited when Mrs. Korthaus brought us on a trip to see *The Lion King* on Broadway—at least once a day, I'd say to myself, *I can't believe this is my life.*

These were prayerful years. At lunchtime or after work, I'd maneuver my way past the tourists on the cathedral steps, lay my handbag on the security guards' table to let them poke around in it, and quietly make my way to slide into a pew. With my forehead in my hands I'd pray: *Thank you* and *Please guide me*, both in the same breath.

I needed that guidance. As exciting as it was, I was realizing that to make it in New York, you had to be the best of the best in the world at whatever you were doing. Mrs.

Korthaus's instruction to *achieve and be an overachiever* was synonymous with the line from "New York, New York": "If I can make it there, I'll make it anywhere." To succeed in New York, first you have to learn to survive. If you make it past that point, then you know you've got real talent.

I quickly learned that entry-level salaries in publishing don't match the rent for a Manhattan studio apartment... but I was determined to earn every penny of that paycheck. To make it work, I'd keep my weekend shifts at Bloomingdale's.

I'd barely sleep that first year, and the pub that opened around the corner from my apartment didn't help when it turned into a nightclub that stayed open until four a.m. For lunch, I often paid two dollars to the hot dog vendor on the corner, but somehow, I always had just enough money to get by. The struggle was worth it: Every morning I walked inside the Rockefeller Center office of a publisher whose name I'd seen printed in some of my favorite books of all time. I wasn't the kid who shied away from growth anymore. This was the biggest chance of my life.

Every day I had to prove I had the chops. Most of my young colleagues had grown up in Manhattan or the greater suburbs, and that seemed to give them an air of calmness I'd need to cultivate. If they felt as frantic as I did about hanging on to this opportunity, they were too cool to show it.

You can play their game.

I'd scurry down the office hallways to distribute the

hotly awaited new manuscript of an author I'd grown up reading; I'd stay late every Wednesday evening after the coming Sunday's *New York Times* bestseller list was released to publishers so I could prepare the packet of sales reports for all the leaders to review before Thursday morning's sales and marketing meeting. As I distributed the packets around the company on Wednesday nights, the glow of the skyscrapers shining through the windows kept me company in the halls of the office building's top floor, where the CEO and president sat. First thing Thursday morning when all the executives had gathered in the conference room, it was my job to use the conference phone line to dial in the half dozen sales reps who worked remotely and merge them all onto the conference line— which immediately taught me one reason New Yorkers are known for wearing black: At work, there are so many tasks that make you break a sweat with an audience looking on.

Even these impossible moments were glorious in their own way, and in a way I couldn't have expected, it felt like home.

"Hey," I'd say to my boss, appearing in her doorway. "I had this idea, and I'm just wondering what you think."

"What's up?" she'd ask me, even though every afternoon she had a train to catch back to the suburbs, where her husband worked from home, to pick up her daughter and son from school.

Maybe one of the reasons working in books felt like a natural fit was because my school years had accustomed me to learning predominantly from women. Now I was coming up in an industry with a lot of female leaders. They worked together to plan book campaigns with creative intuition. Getting things done took finely orchestrated collaboration. They had the smarts to make the kinds of decisions that reach a wide audience and were strong enough to execute on those decisions.

Learning from them showed me that while I wasn't raised with the thick skin of a city kid, my Catholic school experience had given me a strong advantage in the world—in the workplace—by raising me to show my leaders an inherent respect. I found that I knew when I should stay quiet and let the executives speak, when I'd add value to a conversation by offering an idea, when was the moment to show composure, and when was the moment to race down the hall in a hurry.

When I learned a group of teachers from back home was thinking of traveling to New York to see a show, I couldn't help but think of bringing together my mentors at work with some of the teachers who'd brought me up. Many of those teachers were in my mom's book club, so I knew they loved books. Some of them had taught me from first grade through junior high.

I had an idea to take them on a tour through our offices. Wouldn't it be neat for teachers to see how books were actually made? When I presented the idea to my boss, she gave me the thumbs-up to plan it.

When the group arrived in our office lobby, Mrs. Korthaus wasn't with them. She'd been consumed wrapping up the spring musical. Of course she had.

Stepping onto the elevator, the ladies moved in cautious

awe through our building, enthralled as I'd been. I'd reserved a small conference room and arranged for two of the most famous children's book editors I worked with to present my hometown women with a talk about the publishing process. I sat listening to the group's questions, appreciating their appreciation.

"Look at all these *books*!" whispered one as we passed a hallway shelf stacked with titles on our way to the elevators to exit the building.

"Go ahead," I urged her.

"You don't mean we can just...*take* them," said another quietly.

I nodded—and then heard: "*WHAT* are you doing?" One of my coworkers peered out from her cubicle. Another joined her.

"I'm letting them take home books."

"Those are our *publicity* copies!" she whispered.

I glanced back at the group, who were clutching stacks of books to their chests and reading the marketing descriptions on the inside flaps or back covers before sliding more copies into their bags. "This *is* publicity."

"Learn, think, be exposed to all, take advantage of all," Mrs. Korthaus had told me. I was following her instruction, but the *taking advantage* wasn't just for me. When famous authors came in to autograph books, I'd send copies to teachers back home or gift them to the guards who worked in the lobby and couldn't leave the security desk to get books signed for themselves. "You're not from around here, are you, kid?" my favorite security guard, Leonard, liked to rib me.

What gave purpose to the dream I was living was being able to share it with people who had invested in me. I wanted my parents to feel thrilled about the life they'd helped me create. I wanted my teachers to know how far their influence had catapulted me. I wanted young people back home to know that the stories we'd grown up only seeing on TV were within reach for our own lives. Brushing with celebrities, running in heels to catch cabs, collapsing into the conference room chair in relief when the sales reps were all finally patched into the conference line to start the Thursday-morning meeting: These silent celebrations were for everybody I loved. They were proof of what was possible when a girl is raised by people who believe in her.

Most of all, publishing was *mine*. I hadn't known anyone in, or anything about, the business, but I'd found my way. Nothing had been handed to me; I had no family connections. Every task forced me to get better. And, even on the hard days, I did. This was what it felt like to have a career. I had something that was all mine, a way to fulfill myself while also participating in the world. It had its high-pressure moments, but I found it was nothing I ever needed to be scared of. One of my early career mottos was *There's a solution for everything.*

All this inspired me to consider that maybe there was an even bigger world I was ready to explore. After work, I'd start up Fifth Avenue alongside the eastern edge of Central Park for the two-and-a-half-mile walk home to my apartment. Sometimes I walked with a book open, being mindful not to trip on the cobblestone path, my head down as I read. Other times, I simply walked listening to my thoughts, allowing my surroundings, this existence, to absorb into me so it would stay with me forever. Living in New York in my twenties had given me space to make mistakes and still see I could be safe, and to learn on my own what would happen if I made choices I'd never seen a woman make before. When I started using a credit card, I learned why my dad had warned me not to. I made friends at the neighborhood pub. I went on dates with an Australian who'd just moved to New York, a Spanish guitar player, a waiter I'd met at a cafe in the West Village. It was my early twenties, the first time I could learn about the world outside of school. I wanted to take every chance, every invitation, and make every (safe) mistake, so that one day when I found a partner and settled down, I'd never wonder what I'd missed out on.

Four years to the day after I'd moved to New York—the same time span as a high school or college education—it was time to graduate myself from that chapter and all it had taught me. I left New York to move to Europe, committing to at least a year there. This small-town girl who'd once planned never to leave home now longed to be a citizen of the world. I wanted to learn for myself that a woman's life has no limits.

There are some ideas that we can't teach, that we can only try to model in our own lives. One is that love is a beautiful and heartbreaking part of life. It's important to grow and know where you're headed before starting a life with someone.

—Mrs. Humes, high school counselor in Pennsylvania

CHAPTER SEVEN

THE CONFLICT

THE ORGAN IS STARTING BY THE TIME MY MOM AND I find a parking spot and a place to sit in the church, squeezing into our pew on the September Friday morning of Tom Korthaus's funeral. Mrs. Korthaus was just three weeks into the new school year when her husband had collapsed with a heart attack at home one morning shortly after she'd left for school.

He had always seemed enlivened by his wife's energy. I remember he'd gotten a charge out of watching me, the neighborhood kid, in the school theater productions she directed. He'd been cherished in our business and golf communities, and many of those friends and associates are here . . . but scanning the rows of young people wearing navy blue school blazers inside the church, it's clear that the majority of the crowd is made up of Mrs. Korthaus's students.

Tom's job as a national grocery chain executive had brought them to our quiet western Pennsylvania community. They'd moved almost immediately after their wedding in the early 1980s, and true to her nature, Mrs. Korthaus didn't stay under the radar to demurely acquaint herself with the ways of our town. Instead, she started up a catering business after swiftly discerning that our market needed a touch of elegance. When the going got tough for her upscale aesthetic in a town that for the most part didn't even know what capers were, she did the only thing more daring than opening a gourmet hospitality business in a small factory town: She came to teach English to high school kids. Back then she probably couldn't have predicted that thirty-five years later, in the moment she'd find herself on her own in the world, this sea of young people would be the ones to surround her as her family.

Or maybe she could have, because belonging is just who she is.

When the buses carry the kids back to school in time for the lunch period, my mom and I join friends and neighbors at the country club where Mrs. Korthaus is hosting a luncheon. Even in mourning she's the center of the action. It's not as though she's unfazed that her husband is gone—in fact, there's an air of graceful awareness about her. Instead, it's as if displaying devastation would dishonor the loving-kindness that had brought them together to begin with.

As she mingles and greets her guests from table to table with a glass of Chardonnay in her hand, only she could be so clear-eyed in a moment like this: an air of gratitude for the thirty-five years she'd had with him while simultaneously seeming to know that starting now, she'll have to embrace life in a new way.

Each time I walk the dog past her house that weekend, her driveway is filled with cars—her three stepkids', her siblings' from down near Pittsburgh, all most likely helping her square away business and making sure she's okay.

The following week, she's back to school during the day, coaching the mock trial team in the evenings, then back at the country club for dinners with friends. On a Saturday afternoon, I ring her bell to ask if she'd like help pulling her outdoor furniture inside before the cold weather hits.

"Well, sure!" she says. "Come on in!"

I look around at her end tables and bookshelves, how the framed pictures of her and Mr. Korthaus on their beach and ski vacations have a different feeling now. Her house always has that quiet, cushioned feeling, with a freshly vacuumed nap across the carpet and sports or *60 Minutes* on the TV. Together we haul her umbrella table and several wrought-iron chairs down her basement steps. "I was just watching some golf," she says. "Sit down; you want to visit?"

"Sure."

"You know, for thirty years, I grew and prospered in

the hospitality industry." Both her words and her stroll to the wet bar in the dining room make me wonder where she's heading with this. "I was responsible for business meetings, conferences, and conventions at Seven Springs," she says, referencing the popular ski and golf resort as she emerges with two wineglasses and we each take a seat on one of the two loveseats that form an L shape in her living room. "I consulted for universities like Cornell and had a general operations team that provided the very best service possible to our guests."

She tells me how she'd spend the next twenty years there, handling well-traveled clients as the sales and marketing director. "When I went to work at Seven Springs, I didn't need money. My room, my meals: Everything was provided. That was wonderful. Then I met Tom. Did you know this? Tom Korthaus was my customer." The way she names him makes him sound like an institution. Which any man would need to be with a partner like her.

"How old were you when you two got married?" I ask her.

"Thirty-nine!"

"God knew that if He intended you to marry, He had to plant a man directly at the resort."

"You know, I never thought of it that way, but you might be right."

I'd known Mr. Korthaus for about as long as I'd known his wife, and while he was easygoing and uncomplicated, it dawns on me that I didn't know much about what he used to do. She shares how as VP of sales, Tom often planned meetings and trips for his company and clients. Then he booked a conference at Seven Springs. Mrs. Korthaus tells me, "I oversold the resort, as I sometimes did, knowing that shrinkage always happened and that things would work out. Well, when we were overbooked, Tom said he had to come up to the resort himself. 'Where's that sales girl who's been horsing me around on the phone?' he said. So I met with him and was obviously persuasive. I made him comfortable with my arrangements. He said okay, but he wanted me there for all functions to be sure they went smoothly. I was supposed to be in Albuquerque to bid a convention, but he was adamant that I make myself present, and besides that, we needed someone to emcee a dance in the town social hall that weekend. So I went to Albuquerque for one day and got back in time to attend all his functions and call the square dance."

She goes on. "So he asked me to play golf with him. We bet: He gave me a stroke a hole—on my golf course, mind you—and it was too generous. I beat him and then served him a center-cut bologna sandwich."

"Sounds decadent."

Golf handicaps and cold cuts aside, their courtship was a whirlwind.

"His wife had died, and I met his three children. We brought them to meet my family for the traditional Italian Christmas festivities." After they married, they both stayed involved in their corporate careers.

Mrs. Korthaus says, "Things looked pretty good until his company said, 'Okay, Tom, your next move is to Des Moines.' It was not what I expected, but I had made a deal, and I would live up to it."

Metaphorically, she'd been in the driver's seat of her life. When Tom came along, she scooted over to ride shotgun while her career took a back seat. If her new marriage determined the direction for her life, it was because she was cheerfully willing to take her own hands off the wheel. She'd established her identity. Marriage didn't define her. When she got to know Mr. Korthaus, she'd met a man who brought goodness and kindness to add value to her life.

"I'm not getting married until I meet someone who makes me happier than I've made myself," I tell her.

"You've got the right idea."

They stayed in Des Moines for only six months "until it became obvious that neither of us was happy in the Midwest," she says. "Meanwhile, a company had been soliciting Tom to be VP of sales and markcting, so when we came back to Pennsylvania over Christmas, we visited with the executives and decided to return here. It was a good move for Tom and a new opportunity for me." She says this was her time to focus on family, and it would be fun to make friends in our lake and golf community. Plus, moving to our area meant she'd be able to cheer on the Steelers again.

What I'd never known was that when they met, she was just out of a relationship that had been on and off for two decades.

"When the resort grew," she says, "I became the sales and marketing manager, and the love of my life was the head of general operations."

The love of her life: It's a hint of a past I've always

assumed she must have had before she got married. "Eesh, when I think about it: He and I had started working there together when I was eighteen."

"How long did it go on?"

"Until I was thirty-nine."

"More than twenty *years?*"

"It was torrid, but I learned a lot about business," she says. "He and I would argue because he would do and think one way, and I would do and think the other. I was eighteen when we were intimate for the first time. I was of the belief that kind of commitment was forever—which, my heavens, is a very convoluted, complicated thing."

It was the message society had perpetuated about sex in her generation. It's still alive today, the message about being a girl: that when we experience—or even are just curious about—physical pleasure, we have forever given up our worth and power. That's a message that has suited the most insecure of males, and decades after this woman in her eighties navigated what her value truly was, we're still trying to teach girls that our strength is actually in our ability to make the choices that we'd once believed we needed a relationship to help us achieve, like buying a house, traveling the world, or having children. Creating the life she wants under any circumstance is what makes a woman whole.

Mrs. Korthaus was blindsided when Bob proposed to another woman, who happened to adore Mrs. Korthaus so much that she made her a bridesmaid in their wedding. It's hard to imagine that kind of physical proximity, standing as a witness to the love of her life as he committed his future to someone else.

I'm her student, indeed. With this story, she takes class to another level.

She continued to remain sincere friends with the newly-weds, who included her among the group they loved to travel with. A couple years after their wedding, during a ski holiday in the mountains, their newborn daughter, who'd been born with a congenital heart defect, suffered a cardiac event. Turning to her lifeguard training from more than two decades prior, Mrs. Korthaus administered infant CPR as they awaited emergency airlift. By the time the medics arrived, the baby was gone.

"That little girl died in my arms," she says.

After a beat it dawns on her to glance my way, as if to check on me.

All I can do is stare into the face of this woman I've known for so long, and yet have only just met.

"Oof," she says. "That's what we'd call 'gobsmacking,' right?"

Forging one's own life path doesn't mean we will get everything we want. The silent strength is the willingness to carry on in gratitude for all that has gone peacefully.

"I'll tell you," she says, "back then we lived hard, we partied hard, and none of us were prepared for the life that we were living. So in truth? Tom saved me. And I loved him for it every moment of his life."

A career in teaching isn't an easy path. A job that's centered on caring means there's adversity and heartache. What's important is that we overcome it. I left a school I called home for a decade and then returned close to a decade later. Today I am moving forward stronger than ever—because it's not for me. It's for my students.

—Mrs. Snyder, high school art teacher in Pennsylvania

CHAPTER EIGHT

TRAGEDY

THAT FALL, THE COLD COMES EARLY AND THREATENS school delays when the sun melts the snow into morning ice. After the garbage truck drives away on Tuesdays, my dog and I walk Mrs. Korthaus's empty trash cans from the curb to the outside of her garage. "That's you who's been doing that?" she asks me, pausing to roll down the window of her Subaru one morning on her way to school.

"Be careful out there."

My birthday is on the first day of winter, which I always take as a good reminder that during the darkest months of the year, you have to create your own joy. Figuring that this year Mrs. Korthaus could use some too, I email an invitation to a holiday kickoff party at my house, planned for the Saturday night of Thanksgiving weekend. It will be Mrs. Korthaus's first holiday season as a widow.

But on Thanksgiving eve, after we've all been out for the traditional night of homecoming at our beloved bar at the ski lodge, my friend Hope is killed in a car accident. A couple of us had begged her to sleep over at one of our houses at the lake—"We'll wake up and make cinnamon rolls and drink coffee while we watch the parade on TV," I'd pleaded. Hope was twenty-seven, working full-time at a doctor's office and doing hair on the side to fund her studies to become a counselor to military veterans. Instead of staying with us, she'd been insistent on going to another party to see a friend who'd just gotten home on his leave.

I'm at my parents' house with the parade on the TV, helping to set the dinner table, as my friends and I text **lol** because we'd assumed Hope must have had a good night since she wasn't responding, until a friend of my mom texts to say she's just heard the news: Just after midnight, Hope had hit a patch of black ice that caused her car to flip and hit a tree.

At dinnertime, I have no appetite. My extended family, who briefly met Hope at our lake house in the summer when she and my brother went out a few times, politely express their sympathy.

I leave early and walk home...then late that night when I can't sleep, I remember I need to send out an email to call off the party. A good handful of guests respond to my cancellation to express their understanding and condolences, but in all the activity around losing Hope, I don't keep careful track of who's acknowledged that they've gotten my email. I haven't slept in two nights and know that I won't make very exciting company after attending her funeral Saturday morning.

Then, at seven o'clock Saturday night, right when the party was originally scheduled to start, I hear a knock on my front door. I open it to find Mrs. Korthaus on my porch, wearing a Christmas sweater and snow boots. "Merry Christmas!" she cries, shaking a shiny bag. Her hostess gift. "Looks like I'm the first one here?"

The face of faithfulness.

"Come on in," I tell her, trying to sound casual.

"But," she says, "you're... in pajamas. Wait... it's tonight, right?"

In response, I find myself taking in her cheekbones and jawline, her face free of makeup perpetually demonstrating how unflinching she is against life. In all my distraction, it hadn't even hit me that she might not check her school email over the Thanksgiving break. *Why didn't I call her?*

I can hear how ineloquent I sound, exhausted, overwhelmed, as I try to explain what's happened. In insistent response, she turns around to leave. "You get some rest!" she says, handing me the gift bag anyway. I peek inside and find a stuffed smiling toy soldier Christmas ornament with a bell dangling from his hat—cheerful and ready for a party. I want to beg her to come inside, though I'm too drained to muster much convincing. She's worried about me; I'm worried about her. All in the same moment I need time with her...I need rest...I need to know she's not alone...I need to know we'll both be okay.

She continues to rebound gracefully from my mistake, bracing the railing to make her way back down my front steps toward her car. "Let me help!" I insist, holding my elbow under hers in an exchange that twists my heart even more. In the glow of my porch light, I watch her follow my front stone path that's unsteady even when it's not near-freezing in the dark.

What crushes me even more is the part I can't tell her: I feel like I'm not just sending her back home, in the night, alone. It's that, now, *alone* is the way she's living. In just the two months since Mr. Korthaus passed, so much has happened that's provoked my thoughts about how finite, how fragile, this life is. Mrs. Korthaus and I haven't talked about my truest worry for her, and I can't help but wonder whether it's a fear for her too: For someone who has given so much of her life to others, there's a chance she could be by herself as the end of her life draws nearer. Isn't dying alone the most desperate notion that we as women are supposed to fear? I'd like to think I can prevent that; I like to intend that she won't—but what's happened with Hope proves that whether you're in your twenties with your whole future ahead of you, or in your eighties fighting a potentially terminal illness, there's a chance that any one of us could find ourselves alone in that moment. Have we lived to the fullest? Have we come at life with a bustling willfulness to experience everything we can and serve everyone we love? And most of all, have we made our life decisions *not* based in that fear, but instead running with open arms in the wind to embrace whatever comes? Maybe being alone in that moment is not the most tragic thing. Maybe the saddest thing is to spend our years surrounded by relationships that leave us *feeling* alone.

That winter, I'm reflective, like the sunlight that hits the snow on my afternoon golf course walks with the dog. In the mornings I rise while it's still dark to make coffee and open my laptop, doing most of my work before the dawn turns the sky pink between the bare tree branches. I've taken after Mrs. Korthaus when I, too, officially adopt a habit of keeping my nails permanently short. For the first time, I allow what I've spent a lifetime fighting: I let myself gain a little weight. I'm learning that to focus less on my perfection is to focus more on my contributions. I'm letting my role in the world, my writing, start to shape who I am on the outside.

I keep my wardrobe simple and comfy—finding that the older I get, the more I miss how school uniforms always allowed us to focus on function instead of on fashion— and step out only to take the dog for long walks on the golf course, often with my pajama pants tucked inside my snow boots. The expanse of white hills and the bracing air have a way of clearing my head. Mrs. Korthaus, Hope, me: A woman on her own can feel like a balloon in danger of being blown by the wind into the sky above her. At times, I think, it would be nice to be tethered to something. Someone.

I realize a couple weeks have passed since we've seen each other in the neighborhood, which isn't terribly unusual during Pennsylvania winters... until my mom informs me she heard Mrs. Korthaus totaled her car on the way to school. "You're home?" I ask her when I call.

"I'm home! I'm fine," she sings. "Mike Skraba came and took care of me." Mike Skraba is the dad of two kids who graduated back when my brother and I did; he manages the service department of a car dealership that's owned by another family from school. These are the kinds of forever bonds a teacher like her has.

Sunlight lingers longer in late winter when I approach home at duskfall. In her red parka, Mrs. Korthaus is easy to spot, like a cardinal in the snow. She's been getting out regularly to walk on her own—more evidence of her determination to stay upbeat in these gray months. "Hey!" she always calls out the moment we're in each other's sight. Sometimes we chat for just a few seconds to stay in motion in the cold; other times we stop and properly catch up. One day I notice she appears to have a new companion at her side. "Who's this?" I call, studying the little white shih tzu that's prancing alongside her.

"This is Lizzie!" she hollers as we approach. "One of the families at school was volunteering at a rescue, and this little gal needed a family."

"And you're it?"

"I'm it!"

Soon I start to notice that she and Lizzie are passing my house, or we cross paths on the road, just ahead of dinnertime. "Lizzie's forcing you to get out and move before spring comes, isn't she?"

One afternoon on the road, she comes to a very deliberate stop. "They found cancer again."

No. "Where?"

She motions to the general area of her bust. "Just in the one," she says, "so I told the doctor: 'Take 'em both!'" In characteristic animation, she throws up her hands. "I don't need 'em!"

"Can I come with you for the procedure?"

"Too late!" she says. "Already done!" In a single move, she unzips the top half of her coat and yanks it open. Even though she's wearing her oversize Cardinals baseball sweatshirt, I can see the surface beneath is entirely level. *But...why wouldn't she tell me so I could help?* "Now all they've got to do is keep an eye on the part that spread to my spine. Vertebra T-five," she says, parroting the doctor's expertise. "They've got me on an oral medication to keep it under control."

A car passes on the road between us. When she notices my expression, she stomps. "Now you listen," she says sternly. "I flat out *refuse* to be a martyr or a fatalist about this. Okay?"

I stand silently.

"Don't you worry: I'm not gonna be ready to pack it up for at least another ten years."

I've pursued a career, I've achieved what I set out to— all like she once pushed me to do, but by its nature, my work has isolated me. I think part of what she wanted us to learn is that it's in having people all around us that we feel our greatest purpose.

EARLY IN THE SPRING, I HEAR FROM TARA—A FRIEND I grew up with who has become the high school social studies teacher and happens to teach just down the hall from Mrs. Korthaus.

I've been encouraging one of my sophomores to explore her writing, she texts. **I see a lot of potential in Maggie, but she needs someone to help her with her passion. Would you have time to meet her?**

Asking me to step in as a hometown kid's hype girl is like asking a doctor to assist with a medical emergency mid-flight: *Use me!* Where we're from, that's simply what we do, especially because I believe I'm picking up on some code language in Tara's message: When a teacher says they see "a lot of potential" in a girl, what that teacher probably means is, "But she needs help seeing it in herself."

When I sign in to the school office's guest book, I find Tara had given me a good read of this sweet, humble, unassuming girl. Would a few minutes together make much of a difference for her?

The timing is interesting. In the winter, my work started to take so much focus that I'd begun thinking about hiring a young assistant, someone who'd be interested in some cash and the chance to learn about publishing and the media, and who'd provide some very light support with my projects, chores, and errands.

"Do you know Maggie?" I ask Mrs. Korthaus.

"Oh, yeah! Good kid. Very creative, really sweet. She loves to read. Hey," she says, "maybe you can bring her out of her shell."

We, as teachers, cannot teach the same way we did ten or twenty years ago. Cognitively, today's students have developed differently than students of the past. They learn best by doing. They need to become comfortable with being problem solvers. Keeping students excited to learn has challenged me to change my teaching style.

—Mrs. Kramer, K–12 technology teacher in rural Pennsylvania

CHAPTER NINE

CORRECTED

THE TIME WITH MAGGIE BRINGS ME OUT OF MY SHELL. By summer, my house is no longer a quiet cabin for solitary work and hibernation. Three more young women have come on board to help the two of us manage through what has quickly become a fast-paced workload. Sidney is home from college in Chicago, Noori is spending summer break from the University of Pittsburgh at the lake with her aunt and uncle, who are friends of mine, and Meagan is the daughter of my mom's good friend and also niece of Miss Graffius, my seventh- and eighth-grade English teacher who held a party in class the day Meagan was born.

Starting back then, in the nineties, Miss Graffius also became an advocate for technology and made a push for the school to start offering more computer-based courses. It seems Meagan inherited that interest—with a computer science degree, she's an ace at anything that involves technology, the computer, or data, which, in publishing, we refer to often.

Noori and Sidney both study communications, so along with Maggie, they help me with research, some more data, and they type out transcriptions of my client interviews. As a team we're managing seven book projects, all in different stages, with clients like a convicted murderer who spent three decades in federal prison and the fire chief from the California town with the highest crime rate per capita after he suffers a traumatic brain injury on the job that forces him to retire. Every project requires a different kind of sensitivity and understanding of social issues, psychology, morals, faith, and people.

The humanities.

The girls follow my lead, keep their heads down for answers, and quickly pick up what I've considered one of the earliest lessons of my career: to write everything down.

I bring on a bookkeeper to keep the finances straight. I learn we've generated a surplus of income that makes it possible for me to update my bedroom, which is on the basement level and opens out onto a peaceful little patio space and a full view of the backyard with the sounds of golfers teeing off and laughing just beyond the trees that border my property. I'd bought it with dark wood paneling, an old gas fireplace, and carpet that had survived humid summers with the house closed up. The girls help me pick an icy paint color to brighten the space up.

One of my client projects requires me to drive up to New England, where I learn that the rescue facility my dog came from is shutting down and they have one more dog left to place. I pick up Harley on my return home, and instantly we're a family of three.

The house is buzzing—sometimes literally, when Eric, my contractor, runs the bench saw in my basement bedroom. On days his daughter doesn't go to camp, he brings her along. For a kid in grade school, she's fierce with the tools and breezes right into position anywhere her dad directs her to take over. I stand aside when she marches through the house with supplies.

Like the college student who can make themselves at home anywhere, Sidney brings along her breakfast to eat instant oatmeal from a cup while she works. Noori joins her at the dining room table, making notes and tapping away at her laptop. Meagan comes and goes from errands, and Maggie jumps in wherever she's needed—sometimes just to take the dogs on walks or to play outside. One day, Harley, the little speed demon his name suggests, escapes when Eric is carrying supplies through the front door. Maggie and I run out to look for him. "Let's split up," I tell her. "You've got to call his name. *Harley!* Call him," I urge her. "*Harley!* Maggie, yell!"

Later, this moment will stand out to me. When she'd first come on board with me, Maggie sat in my dining room while her mom and I had a phone call so I could assure her that her daughter was in trustworthy hands, that I'd even completed my child abuse clearances because I sometimes went to give talks about writing and publishing at the area schools. When we'd finished that call, Maggie quietly asked if there was something she could tell me.

"I just want you to know," she said, "that sometimes I get really bad anxiety."

That seemed to be a growing theme among kids these days. "If there's ever anything I can do, you just let me know. Okay?" She nodded. "Trust me, I know life can be stressful."

Ultimately, Maggie's the one who finds Harley. Two ladies had seen him wandering and put him in their truck. When they spotted Maggie searching with an empty leash in her hand, they knew Harley belonged to her. "They'd picked him up and said he rolled over like a pancake and showed them his belly when they slowed down their truck," she says.

I'm twice her age, with a lot that I packed into the years after I left high school. "Call him," I'd begged her, but I realized there were almost two decades of life experience that made me unafraid to yell my lungs out myself. But she wasn't wrong. There was more than one way to find him.

One afternoon when we're the only two in the house, I wander into my laundry room and find Maggie sitting on the floor against the cold cinder block wall. "This is what happens when I have a panic attack," she whispers.

"Do I need to call for help?"

She shakes her head.

"Want some water?"

Faintly, she nods.

After I race upstairs to get a glass, we sit together in silence until she says she feels calm enough to move upstairs to the couch.

"What triggered it?" I ask her.

Weakly, she shrugs, as if to tell me, *Nothing. Everything.* *Being a girl in 2018*, I tell myself. That's what caused it.

"I'VE NEVER SEEN IT LIKE THIS BEFORE," MRS. KORTHAUS tells me one day when we're out walking our dogs. "All these kids struggling so much. You know I'm supportive of technology and communications," she says. "But these 'smart' phones are some of the stupidest things we've ever done to young people."

"When I was young, adults used to protect us from the world."

"Now what do we do? We put the whole world right in a child's hands."

Back then, we had to pick up a fashion magazine or two that arrived in the mail once a month to dwell on our imperfections. These days, kids can't escape self-criticism anytime they pick up their phones.

Over the next two years, I get to know Maggie and her pack of theater-loving friends who remind me of the group Mrs. Korthaus had gathered back in my drama club days. Maggie teaches me how much has, and hasn't, changed since I was a kid. I thank the heavens that social media didn't exist in my generation—not because Maggie doesn't handle it gracefully, but because I know I could not have.

When someone close to Maggie comes out as gay, I invite the two of them to stay at my house when I go out of town, just like Mrs. Korthaus used to invite us to do, so they can have some space away from the pain and questions of grown-ups. When Maggie's boyfriend breaks up with her, she comes over in the evening to share the same kind of tears and confusion I struggled with at that age. It softens my heart that she finds my presence and my home to be safe and unconditionally loving spaces. All I want is to ease this time in a girl's life and make her feel a little more prepared for what's ahead.

Still, at times our friendship highlights how, even when my intentions are good, I fall short. I'm seeing that part of what made Mrs. Korthaus an effective educator all these years is that she takes neither credit nor responsibility for a student's experience. She fosters, but in a way that's lovingly detached. I feel a lot of responsibility, and I don't have fifty minutes of built-in time inside the classroom to show how much I care. As much as I want to be available to Maggie, my work often still absorbs my full attention—like the time I tell her she's welcome to get dressed for prom at my house, since our nearby country club is the venue, and then I proceed to get so caught up with work and commitments that I'm at a volunteers' meeting in town when she texts me to say she's on my front porch, holding her gown and makeup kit.

I race home. "Just…remind me when we make a plan, okay?" I ask her, crestfallen when she gives me a look that seems to say, *But you're the one who invited me.* She seems to observe that I'm overwhelmed when she takes off to get dressed with friends.

I feel frustrated with myself for feeling frustration with her when I offer her friends my spring landscaping budget to clean up the yard, and instead they spend a week of afternoons celebrating the arrival of sunshine by throwing around leaves as they sing show tunes. (The retired folks in the neighborhood adore the free show, opening their windows to the April air and slowing their cars to listen.)

One of Maggie's friends who joins in happens to be the granddaughter of my third-grade swim coach who'd once had big hopes for me. That perspective helps reinforce for me that they're kids. They didn't sign up to help me manage my grown-up problems. To rescue me, Mrs. Korthaus sends over her student who's started a summer business doing lawns.

When the bedroom renovation is complete with a mini-fridge and coffee machine, Maggie and I make a project of unwrapping the massive new headboard I ordered. We huddle up to read the instructions for how to attach it to my new bed—a California king—across from which Eric has hung the biggest TV I could find, which gets only Netflix and PBS: the only two things I watch. The dogs and I will be living in luxury.

Maggie and I figure out the tools to use. One of us holds all 150 pounds of the headboard steady while the other one works. It takes us two nights, but by the time we stand back, we're staring at a stable, sturdy bed that we've assembled ourselves. "Don't ever let anyone make you doubt that you can figure out anything you ever need to, do you hear me?" She nods. "Women can do anything. High-five."

High-five.

I write a recommendation letter when she starts to apply for colleges and serve as a reference when she interviews for a college internship with a London-based fashion PR agency, which she lands. I'm the only one more dazzled than she is when she decides to spend a summer in France. Going into her last year of college, she accepts a proposal from the close high school friend she fell in love with on a holiday break.

"Maggie's fiancé got a wonderful job!" Mrs. Korthaus is clearly a fan of this young man when we cross paths on an afternoon walk. "They seem very happy."

Hey, wait just a second, I want to say. *You encouraged me to try life on my own at that age!* She'd pushed me to discover the glories of taking the hard road. She was giving Maggie a hall pass!

Should a girl keep herself free to explore the fullness of her own potential, or does joining with a partner make for a doubly full life?

I remember that Mrs. Korthaus once referred to what we do at that stage in life as "tumbling." It reminded me of a toddler in the grass, learning to do a somersault—spiritually limber, free to take clumsy risks and be imperfect and then stand back up and raise her arms in triumph for even having tried. I'm inching toward my forties, still fully certain that the years I spent exploring my life and investing in my career were the right choices...for me. But part of believing in the potential of women is appreciating that each one's life is made up of a series of events based on each one's individual choices.

The month when Maggie is about to graduate from college and then immediately get married, I'm cleaning out my bedroom drawers—which reminds me of the night Maggie and I spent more than an hour sitting on the floor and talking as we paired up all my loose socks—when I come across something she gave me the week before her high school graduation. "Mrs. Korthaus gave us an assignment to write a letter to someone who's made a difference in our life," Maggie said.

I remember accepting the letter, feeling that whether she'd intended it or not, Mrs. Korthaus was assuring me that I'd done pretty okay by Maggie.

Now, I reread it:

> *I am so glad I have had the opportunity to work with you and become close to you. You have been a great help through everything with my life (and my love life). You have become like a big sister to me.*

As her role in the world is about to shift into both a young professional and a wife all in the same summer, reading those words makes me pause. Maybe that's a bigger part of what makes Mrs. Korthaus such an incredible teacher: She's always known there's no textbook that can teach us to genuinely care. She does her best for every student and then gently opens her grip to release them into the world.

There are many of us who have returned to her at certain points over the years, and some who simply remember her dedication and energy. "My life experiences have been different," she tells me. "I've been able to take new risks, learn new things. Whether I was teaching you in the classroom or directing you in a play, I engaged you kids. I didn't try to *teach* you."

Maybe there's some chance I've played more of a role than I'm giving myself credit for...and maybe never knowing for sure has to be enough. Both Maggie and Mrs. Korthaus show me: Any role we play in the life of a young person isn't for us to determine. That part's up to them, in their time.

I've lived believing that everything happens for a reason, even when the reason is unknown. Following my wanderlust to teach on four continents, I was living in Spain when I received a job offer in South Africa—a place I'd fallen in love with while visiting a few years before. I took it as a sign and accepted the job.

I was on safari with a friend when I met someone who ended up being my "reason": Our safari guide from that trip is now my husband. Today, after ten years of marriage and three international moves, we're living our life with our child and fur babies under the African skies. So yes: I still believe that everything happens for a reason. If you open your heart to the unknown, the most beautiful parts of life reveal themselves.

—Mrs. Connelly, kindergarten and elementary teacher in Tanzania, and one of my college roommates

CHAPTER TEN

PRECIOUS

MY FRIEND KEN PAGE IS A WIDELY PUBLISHED RELA-tionship therapist who says that for those of us who have genuinely longed for a healthy partnership, there finally comes a point when we're no longer "sticky" to the partners who don't love us well. We lose our taste for the kind of attraction that's doomed to lead to heartbreak.

Mrs. Korthaus's story about Bob had hit me hard because too many of my own relationships had shown me what it was like to be let down when I'd made my own life choices based on a guy. Though I own my home, for the first time in my adult life, there's a serenity in accepting that I might end up moving into the future alone. It's not what I thought I wanted—but maybe an even greater blessing for a woman than finding love is learning that she can take care of herself. Inner peace is the new sexy. Why not? If I go about life on my own as intentionally as I did when I bought the house, I could be very satisfied. I can adopt a child. I can rescue more dogs. I can think about what it would take to have a baby alone—I'd frozen two dozen of my eggs three months before I bought my house. Isn't that the ultimate strength? Not to need anyone?

I discover God knows there's one area of my life that will get my attention and bring me to my knees. It's the means of a woman's independence: my finances. "You had a good year," my bookkeeper calls to tell me.

"I sure hope so. It was busy."

"We owe twenty-eight thousand dollars in taxes."

"Twenty-eight *thousand*?" I glance at the signal indicator on my phone, hoping his line has just cut out and I've heard him wrong. That's more than the bedroom renovation cost.

I stand at my door, looking out over my backyard. *Nine-tenths of an acre*, I sometimes marvel, labeling all that's mine in the world with that metric—not even quite an acre, but enough for the dogs and me. *Everything inside the fences.*

For a decade I've been self-employed, trying to make clients happy with what I write about their lives while in the next breath politely reminding too many of them that under the terms of our contract, they owed me payment months ago. At times, the stress has felt like it would kill me.

It occurs to me that the only people I've been able to actually count on to help me run my business were those four young women in their teens and early twenties, all of whom I could trust, but all who had their own lives to live. Plus, even aside from my work, I had my personal finances to manage too.

Is all this can-do independence just a story I tell myself? This career, this house, this life: Is it truthfully too much for me to manage?

Working through my options, I call my dad, who tells me I'm on my own. I call my brother, who agrees to co-sign with me on a loan since the bank can't fully trust a self-employed creative professional. My brother has stepped up, which makes me feel less resentful that the boys in the family had everything handed to them when they walked into the family business, but I was always met with discouragement anytime I inquired about entering it myself.

In this moment of lone despair, at age thirty-eight, I realize: *No one is coming to save me.* Ever. It is time for me to accept that I do not have the same advantages as the males in the family, and it is time for me to respond to that with my own determination to truly, authentically establish my own path. I have always been afraid to separate myself because I don't know who I am outside my family, prominent in my small, chatty hometown. I guess this is what I've been asking for: I have no choice now but to find out.

I fall to my knees and rest my forehead on my new

floor—European herringbone; God, it turned out beautifully—as my heartbeat throbs through my throat and temples. Panic. Anger. Resolve. "Please, God," I say, followed by the prayer I made up when I was in my twenties in New York: *Every single thing I do is a little prayer to You.* Every decision I've ever made was out of faith. How had I gotten here? "Please give me the answer."

What comes to me is one word: *Karin.*

Karin?

Our local hospital system has just announced a five-year, $120 million expansion project, and my friend Karin is leading the fundraising efforts. Maybe this was like Mrs. Korthaus's catering business. A decade of self-employment has taught me that working for yourself is not the blissful existence we like to believe it is.

Karin says it's good timing. She needs help developing some fundraising brochures. "You should come and work on the project with me. What are you doing this Friday?"

"What's the date?"

"June twenty-second," she says.

I don't know why it enters my mind that I'll be thirty-eight and a half that day.

"Come and network with some of the new executives," she says. "We have our annual golf tournament."

June 22 is the day after the summer solstice, which means the sun rises early enough for me to take Harley on a run and even do ten minutes of yard work before Karin swings by to pick me up. Pulling into the golf course parking lot by eight a.m., she exclaims, "Oh! Looks like you'll get to meet

Dr. Q, the new chief of quality and patient safety they just brought here last month from California. That's his car."

We find Dr. Q manning the "chill & grill" barbecue area, preparing food for the golfers while dressed in an apron with a hospital-branded black golf shirt—pulled together and sharp—flat-front plaid shorts...and unforgettable bright red Air Jordans.

"My three kids tease me about these shoes." He grins, flipping the hot dogs on the grill in front of him. "I tell them I'm still young! And I'm single. I can get away with being bold."

He's one of those distinguished older gentlemen, and he speaks with a mild accent that's just like Noori's uncle's, from Pakistan, which Noori schooled me is neighbors with India, Afghanistan, and China. "Would you like a hot dog?"

Karin and I bust out in laughter at the innuendo, and he goes on smiling with a certain wit that's both knowing and innocent.

"Well," I tell him, clearing my throat, "I guess eight in the morning isn't too early for a hot dog now that it's summer."

The coincidences are uncanny: Exactly like Mrs. Korthaus, one sunny day on a golf course at the tail end of my thirties I meet my husband—who, like Mr. Korthaus's husband was, is the father of three children.

For years after, he'll tell the story: "I knew that if she turned back to smile at me as she and Karin walked away, that was my sign."

Having no way of knowing this, after Karin has made sure things are running smoothly, I turn back and wave to him as she and I head back toward her car to stop by her office.

Later that day as we socialize back at the country club, I'm trying to discern whether Karin is playing matchmaker when she says, "You should interview Dr. Q for this project for the fundraising brochures." She explains that he's on national advisory boards and is one of the foremost experts in the country on patient safety and healthcare quality.

Mrs. Korthaus, her friends, my family, my friends and family who have little ones: Nobody's impressed that these healthcare executives who are moving in from other parts of the country are expanding our local hospital by building and buying more hospitals in towns that are hours away from ours. What we all want to hear is that our care is getting better right here at home.

I schedule a meeting with Dr. Q. We've needed someone to oversee our healthcare quality for quite some time.

The morning I go to his office to interview him, he meets me at the Starbucks counter in the hospital lobby. Even more impressive than learning there's a Starbucks inside our hospital is his stature. He looks taller than I remember, wearing a dark navy suit, and the cinnamon and spice smell of his cologne has a way of making me feel at home even though he's the one who's new here.

We sip iced coffees, which reminds me of what it was like to be in the world outside my hometown, as I take notes on what he's sharing. When I tuck my notepad into my bag to wrap up, I ask him: "So where are you living?"

"I bought a house at the lake," he says.

"Oh, nice. I grew up at the lake."

"Well, actually, I'm looking for a tennis buddy," he says. "Do you know anybody who likes to play?"

Right away, I know who to text. **Great!** Mrs. Korthaus responds. **There are guys who play Wednesday nights, and some are looking for a partner.**

I give Dr. Q my phone number before he has to run to his next meeting. He invites me to listen to a presentation where he'll launch a new safety initiative of daily morning briefings that will improve patient safety and ensure patients find easy access to care. *If they lead with this messaging, the whole region would buy in*, I think.

We chat for a few minutes after his talk when I subtly notice that he's wearing a pattern of tiny sailboats on his tie. It's as if he's just grateful to be part of our town now. Everything about him is packaged with polish, but with this quiet spirit of celebration about him. He radiates goodness.

When he texts to ask me out to dinner to discuss writing, which he's been interested in doing, I don't know exactly why, but I decline. When he reaches out once more, I agree, but then cancel at the last minute.

Over the years I've heard my friend Ken, the psychologist, deliver different bits of advice that have been transformative for me, but the biggest takeaway he's taught me is this: We might have a list of all the features we want someone to possess, whether it's being tall, or well educated, or funny, or passionate about their career...but Ken teaches the one characteristic that truly matters is *the way they make you feel.*

So when I finally accept Dr. Q's third invitation to dinner, I can't tell if it's his cologne or his aura that I'm breathing inside his SUV. The interior of his car is spotless. He is cheerful, relaxed. He never said this was a date, but I find myself enveloped in a kind of warmth that's new to me, yet familiar. His vehicle trundles over the gravel of my driveway...and I ask myself:

Krissy, you said if you were going to settle down, it would take a real man. Did you mean it?

We go to dinner on the golf course patio, and he orders a dirty martini—my favorite drink, a taste I inherited from my grandpa. He asks me questions about myself, and when I respond with my guard up, as I've grown so used to doing on dates, he gently, soft-spokenly, invites more out of me. He is kind with his responses. He is mature.

On our first date, then our second, he sits back in his chair in a way that makes clear that he's listening when I speak. The ease I discover in opening up to him shows me how beat up I felt from two decades of dating without even realizing it. As we chat, his presence comforts me in a way that feels like a break. All in the same moment, he seems to acknowledge and embrace *and* look past how tough the path I've chosen has been, managing career and my finances and enduring so many heartbreaks.

Throughout the summer, we become a regular fixture sitting outside at the golf tavern. We often bump into Mrs. Korthaus and the ladies in her golf scramble, a couple of whom tease him about how they love to get close just to smell his cologne. "He's sophisticated," one of the ladies whispers. He lovingly humors the attention, but what makes me proudest is how they don't even know how skilled and resolute he is at advocating for the community that brought me up as a child, that I'm now watching move into old age, to receive the medical care they deserve. As time goes on, I see that he's a rare warrior for patients in an industry that is often driven by the bottom line.

For the first time, I'm also beginning to learn the very real side of a serious relationship in some of the ways Mrs. Korthaus and I had only scratched the surface of: what it means for someone to know all of you and love every bit of it. The menopause book we found on her nightstand all those years ago. The outspokenness of her opinions that the community knows her for. I remember how sometimes at night, Tom Korthaus used to slide quietly into the back of the theater during our rehearsals and take a seat. He'd laugh at the funny lines and clap at the end of the songs to help us get used to the presence of an audience and encourage us that our effort was yielding the reactions we were hoping for. It always seemed that was just his way of getting quality time with his wife, never begrudging that he had to share her with her students. In fact, I think that's what he loved about her. By supporting us, he supported what was most important to her.

For years I had dreaded ever allowing someone this close to me. The part of me that had once craved being protected and cherished and adored had built up an outer shell that Q was chipping away at... patiently, lovingly, willingly, without force. I'd never known what it was to be embraced so completely by someone. There was just one problem.

On our second date, he confided in me that while he and the mother of his children had been separated for the better part of a decade, legally they were still married. "I've stayed in it for my kids," he said.

So that was the catch. I responded curtly. "You should really take care of that before you ever try to date anyone. Especially me."

"I see potential here," he said. "I'll prove it to you." He explained that he'd been waiting to meet the right person before he caused upheaval in his kids' lives. I eyed him carefully. I was through listening to guys' words. I'd be watching his choices closely.

Mrs. Korthaus and I are sitting on her deck watching a late August sunset when we discuss this. "It wasn't easy for me," she says. "Tom's first wife had passed away suddenly, tragically. I came into the picture not long after, and I had to tread very, very carefully. Our relationship was very comfortable for both of us—but it would require me to change." Here, she pauses. "Krissy, I don't even know if I could possibly describe a loving relationship I'd ever been in before him, because I'd always called the shots. When I met Tom, it was the first time that I was required to compromise."

She tells me the unconditional love and security in their relationship, neither of which she'd experienced before, made her thankful that she hadn't gotten her way in marrying Bob. "Right now for me, it's lonely sometimes because I don't have any male social life. Not that I want to," she adds quickly, "but a lot of events are organized with couples in mind. I obviously am not included." I think about the many women in my generation, including myself, who know what that feels like long before we're widowed.

"Fortunately," she says, "I'd learned to like myself before I met Tom. You have to learn that your own company is acceptable."

She makes reference to an old friend of hers she says is a devoted wife. "She never took a single college credit in her life; she wanted to be taken care of. And she's very lucky because Henry is respectful of her, and he is very keen to make sure she knows she's appreciated."

"Is this your friend from your younger years whose husband you once told me was known to have affairs?"

"Oh, many!" she says. "She's even caught him in the act. You see, some women *make their deals* as a result of catching some of these men in compromising situations—do you understand me? They say, 'I can live with it, but you're going to pay for it by making sure I have a *very* comfortable life.'"

"I'll give my*self* a very comfortable life, thank you very much."

"That's right. I wasn't looking for someone to take care of me financially. If I needed anything, it was to be taken care of emotionally. And that's what Tom did."

Over the next few years, it's what Q does too, as we take life on together. I stay living in my house, my peaceful place to write and spend daytime with the dogs, as he navigates his divorce, the pressure of being a hospital leader trying to do the right thing for patients during the pandemic, and then his stage 4 B-cell lymphoma diagnosis, which rocks us to our core—and which a couple of his friends are honest enough to warn us has a very real potential to be terminal. The day we find out he's in remission following six months of overnight cancer treatments at the Cleveland Clinic, one of his colleagues texts him to check on him. We soon learn this is a way of setting the stage to lay Q off three weeks later.

"You know how it goes," his boss had once told him with a nonchalant shrug. "In healthcare, quality's the first to go when we need to cut costs."

It's one more challenge that tests us, and while his divorce drags on through and even after the cancer treatments, I allow myself to long for the simplicity of my life before I met him. It was me and the dogs; I'd managed to pay off my debt and now was about a year away from paying off my house. Mrs. Korthaus pipes in, seeing how torn I am. "One of these days, you're going to have to learn to compromise."

Which is worth it when I stop and think of the difference it's made in my life to have found somebody this compatible. This loving. This willing to be the place for me to put my love.

So even in the moments when I feel I'm giving up my freedom, I choose to hang in there with him. We talk about marriage—my family, his family, our future family—and what relocating would look like if his career calls us to leave the people I love and uproot the dogs from the home they've known with me... our nine-tenths of an acre. "Remember what I told you," Mrs. Korthaus singsongs. "You'll have to make a decision. You might not live here forever."

I take in her words, thinking of the things I'd be giving up: the house that the dogs and I love. My proximity to this community and the people I love. My proximity to *her*.

In writing, we say you have to kill your darlings; or another way we put it is that you can't be too precious about your work. Sometimes, a chain of words you love most is the one most in need of deleting. You have to let go of the pieces you've written that you feel belong when an editor judges they're holding the work back from being as good as it truly can be. Mrs. Korthaus is like my editor, encouraging me not to be too precious about the things I love back home and instead to adventure forward to see how life is writing my story for me. "I experienced all those things!" she says. "You know what it's like to be on your own; you've done that. It might be time for you to try something new."

I'd pursued and lived my dreams, but now I'm being invited to consider that what's waiting for me next is beyond anything I can dream.

I was a semester behind you all in college, but in a way, that made me very fortunate because I wound up taking some of my education coursework from the night instructors. These were the professors who were leading their own classrooms during the day, often coming straight to campus after a full day of teaching kids. They weren't teaching us to focus on student progress reports and test preparation. They gave us the real perspective and challenges of teaching, from their experience working day to day in a classroom instead of preparing lessons on teaching theory inside an office. These instructors taught us that the most important thing was rapport: that relationship with the student.

I'm sharing this with you right after Thanksgiving break, when I had to tell my first graders today: "Messy poops on the wall happen, and that's okay. What's important is that you have to tell Ms. Cochrane so that I can take care of it. Now, everybody, go wash your hands."

File that under "Things I Never Thought I'd Say" for a thousand, Alex! These are the things they *don't* prepare us for in college, but that was what my first graders learned today. And that was enough. Life's messy sometimes. That's okay. What they need to know is that they're loved right through it.

—**Ms. Cochrane, first-grade teacher in Virginia,**
and another of my college roommates

CHAPTER ELEVEN

PROFESSOR

We need an English teacher ASAP.

It's a text from my friend's mom who sits on a board for the community college.

Would you have any leads on someone who may be interested? They would need a master's degree in English or a subject relatively close.

Days later, I'm handing out the fall syllabus I've just written to forty new faces who, for the next four months, will be my students. Some seem enthusiastic; others, apathetic; exhibiting levels of commitment that are differentiated by signals like their eye contact and smiles (and the couple of yanked-up hooded sweatshirts that suggest they'd rather be left alone), how far back in the room they've selected a seat, the energy with which they take notes, and of course, their participation. At the end of our first class, a few of them nod, and a handful grin in what appears to be their initial approval of me when I'm able to go around the room with each of their names memorized. By the end of the first class, I want them to know that they matter enough for me to have learned their names.

The college offers two-year degrees in nursing and manufacturing trades, and the English course is part of their core requirements. In other words, the communication of thoughts and emotions through literature and the media appears to be a natural passion for only a few.

The first week, I tell them that it's safe to share only as much about their lives as they feel comfortable doing, and that I'll never discuss background they cover as part of the assignments unless they share it in front of the class first. I quickly note that almost all of them have jobs—at factories, at grocery stores, at our regional hospitals—and a good number of them have kids. I don't tell them this outright, but I pledge to myself not to make their lives more jam-packed with stress and work than they already are.

The state body that accredits the college requires that the curriculum cover a broad range of genres—we're talking medieval literature to eighties sci-fi and fantasy to news and current events—with lessons focusing on grammar and syntax as well as comprehension and composition structure. I don't know what would happen if I don't cover all those bases, but the college dean's son is in my class, which is just one reason I hope I never find out.

In my mind I pledge that if I can send every single student into finals with the confidence that each one will be able to write a thoughtful, correctly spelled, and technically accurate cover letter and résumé, I'll have served them successfully. "No matter which industry you go into, good writing stands out," I often tell them. *Show, don't tell.* I hope my own background serves as a good example, but I don't talk about my career often and very few of them seem at all impressed. With every lesson, I work to earn their trust.

There's learning for all of us. As the weeks progress, I come to sense what it's like to be the instructor some students are drawn to without reservation, what it means to meet students who have given up on having much faith in instruction, and what it is to see students struggling through a situation they believe no one could pull them through even if they were open to it. There's the boy who approaches me with curiously knowing eyes on the first day of class. "Are you related to the family who owns the factory in the middle of town?"

"My grandpa started that; all the guys in my family work there."

"My dad has worked for your family my whole life," he says. We stand there regarding each other for a minute—him almost seeming to say, *Your family has provided for me*, as I want to tell him, *Yours has provided for me, too.*

From that moment on, there's a subtle feeling between us that we too are related.

There's the young couple who always sits in the back—well, *he* always sits in the back and often takes notes and assignments home to his wife, who, as he explains to me in the second week, struggles severely with her mental health.

There's the student who wears a hoodie cinched tight around his eyes and jokes to the class about his past stealing cars, but hands in assignments that show me he needs an outlet to express how he's always felt underestimated and overlooked. I let him have the floor as much as he wants it, hoping he can feel that I see his capability.

There's the young woman who comes polished, takes careful notes, and in a small group discussion shares why she is her grandfather's caretaker: because he rescued her and her dog from an abusive home at the hands of her mother. She's studying science to go into nursing, though I can see how romanced she is by storytelling.

There's the mom of three who works the night shift as a medical assistant in the hospital's neonatal intensive care unit. She's trying to get through the nursing program because she wants to help kids like the teams that helped her teen son, whose battle with leukemia made headlines in our region before he passed away last year. Many of her assignments focus on stories about him, and at times I have to ask the class to excuse my tears. Sometimes she nods off in class from the exhaustion of studying, working, and raising two younger kids, but even when a snowstorm hits toward the end of the semester, she's present—and smiling every day. Through what they share in class and in the context of their assignments, my students let me into their worlds—their families, their pasts, their hopes.

The boy whose dad works with my family is a wholesome spirit, and I can't tell whether he's such an active participant simply out of respect or because he'd be genuinely curious to pursue something related to this field if a paid career in writing or media were more in reach in our area. The way he talks about his dad and grandpa, I imagine he'll spend his life close to home. While we have this time together, I try to fill the room with ideas that make his eyes flash with interest.

Over the semester we do drills to distinguish rules like *it's* from *its* and *there, their,* and *they're.* On Halloween, we play Mad Libs on the board with candy. The former "free car" enthusiast surprises me by leading the class in an in-depth explanation of a full-length fantasy work that's a revelation of his comprehension. They sometimes wince at assignments, but only a couple times do I need to chat with a student about a late deadline.

"I don't know what you're doing in there," the dean says, in a way that startles me, until she continues: "My son came home last night and said, 'Mom, I'll be in my room. I need to write seven hundred fifty words for English.' He's the youngest of all my kids, and I've spent his whole life riding him to do his homework. I have to thank you. I think you're getting through to them."

We read a nonfiction short story by a writer whose older brother breaks his neck one summer when he dives into the shallow end of the community pool and spends the rest of his life in a coma. Mrs. Korthaus never used to tear up over moving material, but I can't help myself. "Guys," I ask them. "Have you ever been in a situation when you've mourned someone who's still alive?" They have no words as I wipe tears.

That day on the way to class, I'd pulled up to a gas station and parked right next to someone I'd grown up with whose mental health and drug addiction in high school cut her off from us. When our eyes met, the connection seemed to pull her out of a daze.

As we chatted, she asked me about someone we both know. "How is he?" she said.

"Still an asshole," I replied, and we both burst out in laughter. After we quieted down, we recognized what was happening. That single moment gave us the chance to feel like even though twenty years had passed, we'd never lost each other.

We write stories, we read stories, so that one reader will feel less alone in their hurt. Their *conflict*. We teach to make sure an individual just knows that these resources of compassion and shared experience exist. If we've done our job, the student is left with an inextinguishable willingness to search for material that validates their lives and reminds them that even when they feel alone, they're forever linked with others.

The only students who don't get As or Bs are the few who blatantly disregarded the maximum of three absences without any explanation. The husband who reports in for his wife gets an A...for them both. I'd struggled with how to handle it, but had finally decided I don't want to be the reason she gives up. If anything, I figure, she deserves an A for the loyal and caring husband she chose.

I'm invited back for a second semester, teaching both English and communications. I accept, even though my evaluations from the students at the end of the semester—*my* report card—contain their critical points. A few scored me low for not always starting class on time. I shake off the truth: They don't realize that I too have a lengthy commute on back roads, sometimes in bad weather. I'm sometimes rushing out the door after developing lesson plans and grading essays and projects in addition to the work I had on my plate before I started here, because if I really kept track of all the hours I spent preparing lesson plans and grading their papers, I'd be earning less than minimum wage. I'm learning these are costs that educators don't count. I'm giving them my best work, just as I aim to do with everything I take on.

Most teachers probably recognize that we'll never please them all, but as I scan the rest of the report, there's the grade I really wanted to see: *I feel that this instructor cares about me.*

It's my highest score.

I believe I treated them all with the same approach—at least I meant to—but there are a few who will manage to stand out. They're the students who, even in their own very quiet ways, were open with me about the struggles in their lives, who were there out of their commitment to work toward a better path, who understood that we get out of life what we put in, and who let me in out of their trust that I would be part of their solution. The ones who believed—whose hearts were still trusting enough to believe—that I cared.

At the end of the semester, the mom of the child who passed away hands me the final yearbook photo of her son that was taken four months before he passed. I pin it above my office desk at home, understanding it's as if she wants me to know that I've been teaching them both.

Teachers are peacemakers in the little world of the classroom. We are the example of true tolerance and acceptance. We have to be the kind of people we're challenging our students to be.

—**Mrs. Shick (again)**

CHAPTER TWELVE

INTEGRATED

I LOVINGLY REFER TO MRS. KORTHAUS AND HER SQUAD as the "ladies of the lake"—the rambunctious group of gals known for being highly social and generous to community causes. After I moved home and started getting involved in the community, a handful of them recruited me to join the board of directors for our free medical clinic. It's an invitation I'm humbled to accept when I join my godmother, Joann, and one of Mrs. Korthaus's close friends who chairs the clinic's committee that plans and promotes our fundraisers.

At my first meeting, I notice some of the men on the board try to still themselves from too visibly squirming in their chairs when I share that as a young professional who couldn't always depend on steady health insurance, I know personally what this volunteer work means in people's lives. I'm not sure exactly what it is about my disclosure that appears to make them uneasy, except that maybe the world often doesn't realize the resourcefulness that's required of a young woman whose own responsibility it is to take care of herself.

The ladies also wrangle me to join the community hospitality committee. We hold our committee meetings at the country club, where Mrs. Korthaus leans back shrewdly in the dining chair with her arms folded across her Hilton Head sweatshirt. She turns every head at the table her way when she thoughtfully raises her finger to share her points. It's the old "Don't raise a problem if you won't propose a solution"—and she always does, and she sits on the board of directors that some of us have heard is talking about shutting down the ski lodge, which houses the most beloved bar at the lake.

Not only in front of students, but also in the broader community, she's never feared being ostracized for being a leader. Discussing a tender subject that can make a group of hometown women feel like we're whining hopelessly, Mrs. Korthaus keeps a steady-handed position on the matter and is somehow always the one with a way of moving the conversation toward progress. When one of them waffles and second-guesses herself, Mrs. Korthaus calls her out. "Oh, Linda. You know what? You have to be the most conflicted person I know." In a small town among the overly polite generation of women, Mrs. Korthaus is the only one honest enough to call out how equivocating, nail-biting, and speculating gets a situation nowhere.

While she can casually shake her head about the changes brewing in the community, I have a harder time brushing them off. It bothers me that one group of old-school leaders wants to throw their weight around making decisions that affect all of us. It appears I have moved back to my hometown at a time when they are starting to feel threatened that the advantages they've enjoyed could be clawed back.

At pub trivia night while Mrs. Korthaus and I chair-dance to Beyoncé when our group gets a question right, from across the room I notice someone who's known my family for years glaring at me. I stare right back, puzzled. Is he feeling threatened because we on the hospitality committee put a vegan burrito on the menu at the golf tavern? Or because the world looks like it could grow fairer for women, and we want to wiggle about it a little to "Run the World"? My bucolic little lakeside hometown has become a battleground of wills.

One Monday night a month I start to attend the community board of directors' meetings—sometimes alone, sometimes taking a seat next to one of the other ladies from the hospitality committee. As one of the directors on the board, my beloved teacher sits with her eight peers behind a table facing us with her name on a vinyl placard in front of her. When I smile and give her a little wave, she remains stone-faced. She's so official.

I listen as neighbors step up to the microphone stand in the middle of the two aisles in our country club ballroom

turned town council meeting format, most of my neighbors speaking with our native Appalachian drawl: "I'm
Sam Campbell, section five, lot a *hunnn*-derd and nine.
I'd like an update on the discussion about boats speeding
on the main lake..."

Then, five minutes later: "I'm Sam Campbell, section
five, lot a *hunnn*-derd and nine. I'd like an update on the
deer-hunting policy, please..." Each topic stirs up conten-
tious debate, with a member of the board eventually stepping up to try to wrap up each discussion "in the interest
of time."

I suppose if I had to pick a side, I identify as part of
the group that doesn't think hunting in residential neigh-
borhoods is wise, and that opposes the sale of lumber
taken from our centuries-old evergreens. Meanwhile I
can't seem to comprehend how one agenda item focuses
on the filth of our lake water while the next discussion is
raised by a group who says they're unwilling to honor the
catch-and-release fishing policy.

"Shut the hell up!" the board president shouts when he
disagrees with any one of us constituents.

I shrink in secondhand embarrassment. *Just let the
poor fish go!* I want to yell. *Who wants to eat anything
that's grown in that water anyway?* I've never seen con-
troversy over such benign topics, such competing interests
among people who care for one another, or such a lack of
civility among adults—especially leaders.

I get mixed reactions when I start to think about running in the annual election to join the board of directors.
The women on the hospitality committee think it's a swell

idea and offer to sign my official petition that establishes clearance to run. My dad is concerned about my image: "You're about to become *very* unpopular," he says.

That possibility doesn't concern me. There's work to be done, and Mrs. Korthaus is one of the only women in the community who's stepping up to do anything about it. But when, for a project, I speak with a young congresswoman whose campaign succeeded in flipping her district for the first time in four decades, she says, "You're running for your community's board of directors? I'd take my job any day before I'd ever do that."

Of course there's one opinion who will be my deciding factor. In the face of a disgruntled, male-dominated small town during a heated era for culture and politics, Mrs. Korthaus urges me to step up and run. "Only if you coach me," I tell her. She's sat on the board multiple times, often taking stances that get the hometown traditionalists' knickers in a knot. She and I both recognize that I face becoming the lone female, non-conservative voice on the board, and possibly the youngest board member in the community's history.

But there is one topic everyone agrees on: the ski lodge. Sitting at the top of the old ski slope that hasn't operated since around the time I was born, the pub and restaurant at the peak have managed to maintain the most popular destination for night life in the region: summer music festivals on the slope that's been converted to an amphitheater, the house band, called the Rum-Dums, whose Tom Petty covers always get everyone on the dance floor, the back deck view overlooking the mountains (and on the clearest summer days a shimmering corner of the lake), and a U-shaped bar that facilitates easy glimpses of the neighbor you realize you've been longing for ages to sit and catch up with over a drink. Any Friday or Saturday night at any time of year, it's hard to find a space to fit in the ski lodge parking lot or dance floor.

That's certainly never truer than the day when the board leaks word that after almost fifty years of operation, they're shutting down the ski lodge tomorrow.

I spent entire winters on the sledding hill out front, running upstairs to the bar and restaurant where my parents, aunts, and uncles had pizzas and hot chocolate waiting for us. When I was six, my babysitter, Susan, taught me to ice skate with the big kids on the old basketball court that the water company would delight us by hosing down so it would freeze over. One summer in high school I worked in the arcade on the first floor, and after we turned twenty-one, the upstairs bar was the one place you could go that you always knew was going to be fun and made for a short walk home. It's one of those places with its own down-home energy that's gathered the most loyal following anywhere.

"They can't close it," I tell Mrs. Korthaus. She shakes her head, which tells me her hands are tied, and she won't be successful trying to persuade her peers on the board anymore. We celebrated her birthday there the year before last. The other board members are relative newcomers, having moved here for retirement or business, finding this sleepy little lake community to be a wildly affordable place to live a waterfront lifestyle that people pay millions to enjoy in other parts of the country. The next night when the Rum-Dums play one final time, people dance on top of tables over a crowd packed so tightly that if a fire were to break out, we'd all get trampled while we tried to flee. The next morning, the dogs and I hike up the ski slope and find that the doors have already been chain-locked shut.

The whole town feels immediately different. This is the first time I've ever noticed that leaders in our community prioritized their own agendas over what's good for the people.

Mrs. Korthaus's term on the board is ending the morning of the annual meeting when the secretary announces the election results. I've won a seat.

"Just listen and learn," my dad suggests, but at the first closed-door meeting that coming Monday night, I feel a responsibility to share my thoughts. Right away, I learn what it's like when people make hurtful comments publicly, what it's like when they make flattering comments publicly, *and* why it's an equally terrible idea to respond either way. Mrs. Korthaus and I pass on a walk, and she's my teacher again: Instead of giving me the answers, she seems to spiritually stand back. "You'll figure it out," she says.

You can play their game.

One month in, it's grown clear what the critics meant about how tough this would be. I keep showing up. I took this on for the community. Those first battles blow over, and I learn to operate with a little more grace. A few weeks in, I find myself in planning meetings with figures like our township director, a county judge, and the fire chief. Sometimes they're asking for my expertise on reaching the community through education and messaging. At times, I'm the only female in the room.

The ski lodge has been closed for a year by the time a couple of friends and I make arrangements to receive the keys to walk through it. Most of the doors were boarded up after kids broke in and sprayed the white powder of a fire extinguisher across every surface. Inside, the old resort pinstripe valances are still hanging over the louvered windows that face the front, and we duck from the bird that's flying around solo in the old dining room.

I talk with the new president of the board, who is more poised and levelheaded than the last. I talk with another board member who was voted in alongside me and who spent his career working in corporate franchising for national restaurant chains. I talk with the township manager and a building inspector who's a family friend to help determine whether we can keep the current building, which I and many of us are, well, precious about, or whether we need to build a new one. "Well?" says Mrs. Korthaus.

I respond as a student who was raised and schooled in faith. "If God surrounds me with the right partners to pull this off, I'll do it."

Within a year of my being elected to the community board, it's through my colleagues on another volunteer board that we gather a group of five young professionals— a few guys I grew up with and a friend of a friend.

Mrs. Korthaus is the one who showed me how to put

on a production, and the one who taught me how to gather a crowd to it. "Oh, prayers answered!" she cries. "This really could work!"

By God, it starts to. We form a business, and I recuse myself from the internal board discussions about the deal. The board publicly opens invitations for bids from investors. We, and one competitor, present our proposals for what we intend to do with the land, and community leaders see salience in our business plan. Next, after approval from the township, for the first time in history the board agrees to sell the property.

Mrs. Korthaus tells me when she was growing up, she used to love leaving the girls' school to participate in activities at the boys' prep school.

"Why?"

"The men just regarded us girls as students." She explains they were more easygoing than the nuns, who were more driven to discipline, and that learning from men promoted her intellect and gave her confidence. "It was about being able to adapt, not to be intimidated," she says. "That's a very big thing. It became even bigger in my early career because I was dealing with men most of the time. I never let that bother me. Every one of the business conference planners were men. I had to make them be impressed by how much I knew and how great I could make their experience. That's probably been my biggest goal: I've been a facilitator. What does a facilitator do? They pull from here, and they pull from there, and they make it work."

I find myself in a similar position as the lone female.

For the past couple years I've taken on more work than ever and have continued taking book projects that I tackle at night and on weekends. It is endless, I am exhausted, but now I have a significant savings. The ski lodge property and demolition will require more than $50,000 cash investment from each of us, and then we win a grant from the state for $1 million. The tri-county newspaper runs a front-page story about us, and the regional news station comes out to shoot a segment on the project. What for years seemed like a hopeless loss is now being championed by the entire region, as well as government officials and the local press.

But then, a few of us notice that the tone among our partners starts to change. There's a sixth partner who wasn't part of the original partnership's conversations, but who's requesting a share of the property equal to ours in exchange for operating the business for us. The majority of us exchange glances and hold a series of conversations about the pros and cons. We're getting ourselves into a mortgage of more than $3 million, I tell myself. My best friend's husband is the executive chef at a historic golf and polo club in the Northeast. He's a hometown kid who went on to win regional chef competitions and prepare meals for US presidents and some of the most recognizable business leaders in the world. He knows our market, he knows the ski lodge, and he's the one I'd been in earlier talks with to helm the menu and all the culinary and creative direction. I'm not comfortable taking on my portion of the mortgage, more than half a million dollars of debt, without feeling sold on the person who will lead the vision for our business.

The majority of us establish that we all see the situation similarly: No one should get a share of the property without investing their hard-earned capital. But the sixth voice manages to stay involved, and the conflict continues: over the logo, the floor plan, even the name. "How many startup restaurants get to buy a brand name and a location that already has five decades' worth of followers?" I point out. "Of all the decisions we need to make, why would we change the name when everyone is just going to call it 'the ski lodge' anyway?" It's not just a building; it's an institution.

Fifty-three thousand, five hundred dollars. That's the amount of cash I have in it, and I'm confounded at how ineffective I am at leading the first passion project I've ever been involved with. It's not that I need to turn a profit. It's that I want to give my community something special in collaboration with partners I love and who love our hometown the way I do. But month after month, I feel my excitement deflating. I've started and finished three books in the time it's taking to get this off the ground. It feels like $53,500 is a lot of money to put into something I'm not fully convinced will fly.

I start to weigh my options, which seem pretty simple: I can stay involved and continue to bite my tongue and lose sleep over where this project will go; or I can call it out, exit the project, and withdraw my money. I have worked so hard to be able to bring this project to life, even aside from gaining the financial means, and there's no place I'd rather invest my money than to give my community something I know they love—that would give us our place to gather again. *And* it was through their connections to me that all the other partners came on board. At times it feels like I'm being pushed out of the project I gathered the first couple partners into.

There's a core group of us who seem to stand together in our view of what's going on and our commitment for this project to happen for the *community*—not for any of our individual investment portfolios. However, for two and a half years, we make almost zero progress toward any glimmer of a ribbon cutting. Some of the community goes into an uproar when they see the old building come down...a moment that shatters me too. I feel like we're rushing the wrong steps and not focused on the ones that really matter. The project has gotten all this publicity and created so much excitement, but we don't have a clear plan or any timeline we can announce. "We need to be communicating." Every time I say it, all I hear is my defeat. As one member of a partnership, it's simply not my call to make.

It reminds me of school projects when Mrs. Korthaus would sometimes place us to work in a group with a partner or two who weren't our favorite classmates. That was her way of teaching us that there are situations in life when you have to put differences aside and work together. I was always a kid who believed in my classmates' strengths. So with warmth, sometimes softening the grit in my jaw, I try. A couple partners and I work to present solutions and create consensus, get us all on the same page, and move the ball another few yards down the field—at least briefly. When we meet at dinnertime, I prepare meals for everybody. "How did you make your roast?" the fifth partner scowls. "You're supposed to sear it first."

I have no reaction except to think to myself how in the family business, my grandparents taught us to feed the people who worked with us. Gathering for a meal is an act of generosity out of one's own pocket, a celebration of gratitude for the resources that buy the food and the people to share it with. It's one of the reasons why, when Mrs. Korthaus and I are together, we're usually eating. Having a meal as part of work is a sign that you choose to be together even outside of the essential business conversation.

Every time I'm slighted, every time another manipulative exchange happens, I keep hoping one of my partners will put their foot down. But when it comes to voicing the truth about how I feel, I know that's no one's responsibility except mine.

"The whole idea of why I succeeded at the resort when I started my career is because I never would compromise," Mrs. Korthaus says. "I was always in a battle with people who were in the restaurant and hotel business. I maintained my position and fought for what I thought was right."

I'm fighting for what I think is right, but what I know is true is that it's wrong to give a partner a share if they're not making an up-front financial commitment the same way we others are investing our cash and when we can't all respect each other enough to find points of agreement so that the project can start. Again, it brings etymology to my mind. I remember the high school musical my senior year when the cast was fighting, a word Mrs. Korthaus used to describe one of the girls I was upset with caught my attention: "She has as much integrity as any student I've ever met," she said.

I think about *integrity*, from the Latin *integritas*: to be whole. When who one professes to be and who one behaves as are integrated and intact.

I can respect others' polite neutrality, yet I can't stay silent. My honesty is precisely why one of the partners wants me out. Even though none of us wants a sixth partner to be involved with no financial commitment, I'm the only one who will say so.

"WHAT'S THE STATUS WITH THE SKI LODGE?" MRS. Korthaus has asked me time and again when we pass each other on walks. This evening I pause in the road and shake my head to tell her, *We're not getting anywhere.*

"Well, what the *hell*?" she says.

My thoughts exactly.

She weighs in with the same kind of tough love she used to give me in high school. "If this whole thing goes under, it's going to be because of infighting between you all." In other words, it's ours to lose, and the community is counting on us.

It takes all my strength not to rebut. But in my heart of hearts, I also know her well enough to understand that she would never want me to enter a situation when I'm putting my entire personal savings on the line. "Five years of tours, meetings, applications for permits, applications for grants," I tell her. "Fifty-three thousand, five hundred dollars. Do you know how hard I've worked for that money?"

At that, she rests her case. As a longtime teacher, she knows about hard work and sacrifice. She knows about values. And she knows about reaching the point when enough is enough. There's not a chance she'd want to see any one of her students suffer a loss over something we undertook with the intention to bring something special back for our town.

"I talked to Josh," I tell her, referring to an old friend since grade school and former student of hers whose family has owned multiple respected restaurant businesses in town for decades.

"What'd Josh say?"

"He said: 'Krissy, if you can get out of the restaurant business with the same amount of money you got in with, it's been a good day.'"

She slumps. It's hitting her. She'd once told me, "I had the catering business for one year until I realized how much work catering was, and how little money you can make for the hours spent on the job." We both know Josh is on the money with his advice.

She uncharacteristically withholds any comment. Instead, she listens.

"So often over the years," I tell her, "you would comment on a decision I'd made. Later I would go, *You know what? Mrs. Korthaus was right. She had the life perspective.* Maybe you even took sides with my parents at the time, but I ended up learning your point. And I hear you right now when you say, 'If this project doesn't work out, it's going to be because your partners couldn't get along.' But this isn't about getting along or not getting along. Because I also *know* that as a woman, you would not want me to go forward with my precious earned savings into something that I feel could end up stabbing me in the back. And even though you're telling me, 'Dammit, we all just want this restaurant and bar back'—and I agree with you, we *all* want it back!—"

She looks on with anticipation.

"—I know deep down as a woman that you would never want me to make this decision that would be unfavorable for my own financial wellness. We both know I have worked too hard and sacrificed too much."

"Absolutely," she says. She's surrendering alongside me. "You're right."

No sound-minded person who has ever worked for their money, including Mrs. Korthaus, would discourage me from the blatant sense in the calculus of this decision.

At a meeting among the cash partners shortly after Q's finished cancer treatments and is looking around the country for a job, the fourth partner suggests I've had "a lot happening in my personal life." That's when I let him have it: I feel he's disregarded what I've accomplished and who I am—me, the person who has led the project and who invited him in. I am so steeped in truth and anger as I talk that I can feel my jaw muscles pulling back on my quivering chin.

Then I look ahead at what's to come. "You call Q and me friends," I tell him. "But I guess in the now *years* that we've been discussing this project, there's something really important you haven't learned about me—which is that nothing in my life is worth losing my inner peace over. I'll get out," I say.

"*You'll* get out?" asks one of the other partners. "What just happened?"

I loved the ski lodge; I knew firsthand why thousands of us loved it. I've led this initiative, garnering support from leaders in the community for a project most people had said would never be possible. This was my dream… and I'm the one exiting.

A month after I make my exit, the source of the problem disappears. But of course—my unwillingness to comply was always a threat, but my guess is that without me there, it became clear that no one else involved in the deal was going to put up with it either.

My family, the board president, Mrs. Korthaus are equally disappointed, but if there's anything I've learned from the challenges I've taken on and the woman I admire, it's that I can't go along with something I don't believe in. Good or bad, that's integrity. And even when the outcome is a letdown, a teacher knows they've done the job when they see a student make a decision based on strong principle. "The boys will do a good job with the project," Mrs. Korthaus says.

I agree. "They will." I'm sorry for myself, but it was always for the community.

Sometimes, the best lessons come from surrendering to life's plan and letting it guide us in unexpected ways…There are moments when the curriculum takes a back seat to the real-life experiences that shape our students. It's in the unplanned that both the teachers and students *often find the most growth.*

—Miss Snyder, elementary teacher in Pennsylvania, daughter to Mrs. Snyder and sister to Mrs. Humes

CHAPTER THIRTEEN

A DOLL'S HOUSE

ONE NIGHT DURING THE MOST PAINFUL PART OF Q'S treatments, I have a premonition dream that I'm at a nighttime party set high on a hill that's surrounded by more hills, and I'm in the company of women I feel are somehow wiser than I am. Looking out across the land with the stars above us, I have a strong feeling: *How am I one of the lucky ones who was chosen to be here?*

When Q takes a job in San Francisco and I fly out so we can find an apartment, I find myself crying as we drive alongside the bay amid the hills. Mrs. Korthaus and my dream were right: There's a new life we're meant to start.

He sells his house. We decide to keep mine, partly so

that we always have a familiar place to stay when we go back in the summers and for holidays, but also because I couldn't let go. I spend the next year flying back and forth for extended visits with him so I can finish a client project in the quiet of the cabin. Sometimes when I go to visit him, Maggie stays at the cabin with the dogs.

It won't be easy, and it will take a year more of his patience before I'm ready to fully relocate. But eventually...I compromise. I take a deep breath before I tell Mrs. Korthaus my decision. My family have one another and can come visit us. Leaving Mrs. Korthaus will be the hardest part of this change.

"Good," she reassures me. "It might be the right decision; it might be the wrong decision: but most important is that it's *yours*."

For weeks Q insists he should take time off work to join me for the cross-country drive, as we've now done twice together with the dogs. But this time, having so many of my belongings permanently packed in my back seat is a reason for me to tell him that for this last journey before we officially merge our lives, I need a final bit of space.

On a Friday afternoon the dogs and I pull out of our driveway to cross through nine states. A few hours after we leave the lake we pass through Ohio, where I went to college, and almost get caught up in a windstorm before stopping for the night just past Chicago. The next morning we ride across the plains and savannahs, passing acres of windmill farms in Wyoming and the eerie salt deserts in Utah. For years I'd taken Interstate 80 from Pennsylvania to New York, and it strikes me how now I'm taking the very same road, but in the total opposite direction of the life I'd created for myself. Each morning on this journey, I get a coffee to go and walk the dogs before I load them into the car with hotel buffet scrambled eggs mixed into their food. We indulge in this last hurrah, just the three of us. The summer sunsets that we follow west invite me to entertain the notion that just maybe where we're headed will be even better than what we've known.

Always mindful to look out for me, Q tracks my location the whole way and each evening calls ahead to make a reservation at a pet-friendly hotel I'll be passing along the highway. We move him out of his apartment, and together we make a down payment on a hilltop house with a detached suite I can use for my office and for family to come stay. I'd worried that I'd miss turning over in bed to look out the window onto my near-acre of trees, but our living room and bedroom both overlook a patio with a view of hills, surrounded by more hills, covered in native Northern California vegetation. The owls call when night falls, and in all the years I lived in the Pennsylvania Wilds, I wanted to see coyotes. Now we watch them wander the hiking trail above us when we wake up on weekend mornings.

He asks me to marry him on a stormy Sunday afternoon at Carmel-by-the-Sea. We say our vows before a female judge on a Friday morning and celebrate by going straight to breakfast at our favorite diner.

Now that I'm away, I find Mrs. Korthaus is much easier to catch on the phone than she'd been for the past eight years. "What are you up to?" I ask when I call her.

"Just watching some golf!"

"You want me to let you watch?"

"No, no." I can picture her in the cushy rocking chair in her living room with Lizzie tucked between her and the armrest. "The question is, what are *you* up to? How's married life?"

"You know what I'm finding?" I ask her. "I like the experience of being married."

"It's something, isn't it?"

"Yeah. I used to want marriage more than anything, and then I accepted it when I didn't know if it would happen. You didn't marry Mr. Korthaus because you needed help paying the bills; you and I had figured out how to manage that on our own. Why did we really choose marriage? I mean, trust me, there are moments when I miss how simple my life was on my own."

"Ha!" she says in apparent self-recognition.

"It's not always easy, and I'm not always graceful about it. But you kept saying it: 'Compromise.' And frankly, I could have done without that part, but there's a growth that comes from that."

"Very much so," she says. "You just got married. I've been widowed, but I'm fine because I was prepared to live however my life ended up, or ends up, being." She pauses and, in her endearing way of moving the conversation forward, says, "It's not exactly the most productive way to live life, getting blotto with the girls at the country club every Monday and Thursday night, is it?"

"Blotto." She cracks me up with the image of her rambunctious crew, tipsy in their booth. "That is such a 'you' word."

"Well, it's true!" she says. "You know, Judy just died."

"I'm sorry, Mrs. Korthaus. My mom told me."

"Things are changing," she says. It's the first time in the thirty years I've known her that she's ever sounded down. "That's why I'm glad we have this project. It gives me something to look forward to."

"You and Lizzie can come out and visit with us this winter," I tell her, feeling like I'm pitching her an article that there's a fifty-fifty chance she'll accept. She'd been down to Hilton Head with friends in late winter and wound up being forced to leave the trip early because she was getting lightheaded. When she told me about it, I noted that for the first time she was letting me see that she was scared. "Q will work with your doctors to make sure you have access to any care or medicine you need."

"Interesting," she says. "I think I'd like that very much."

Well, that didn't take much of a sales job.

We both take a beat—a word that still makes me think of her as she once taught us in a lesson about Konstantin Stanislavsky. It's been suspected that the drama teacher's Russian accent was mistaken as he was instructing his students to take a *bit* of pause. In the silence of this moment, I think how I'd much prefer to keep imagining she'll live forever, but I feel compelled to do what I can to lift her spirits, even from the opposite side of the country.

"You know what I was thinking?" I ask her. "You and I could take a popular work, and you could teach it to me now, the way you taught it to us back in high school."

"Ooh," she says. "Hey, I like that."

"We just have to decide which one we want to cover."

"What about *The Women* by Kristin Hannah—have you read that? Oh, I'll tell you what; it's about the women who were nurses during the Vietnamese War. It's good. Or what about *The Crucible*? It looks like it's dealing with the Salem witch trials, but it's really about McCarthyism. I've developed a whole lesson that I even used for a conference once, and it got a good response."

Oh, this is fun already. Both sound timely, and I remember how much she used to love teaching *The Crucible*. But after we hang up, it dawns on me that there's another work that might hit home even more.

I text her: **What do you think if we do A Doll's House?**

That would work, she responds right away. **I have to read it again. I will start to work on a lesson!**

I know I'm asking her to do some academic acrobatics, as she's told me one of the biggest challenges she encountered that led her to retire: "I can't teach kids through a screen!" Even worse than a screen, I'm asking her to teach me over the phone. When we convene the following Saturday, she doesn't seem to mind terribly.

"I was delighted," she says. "I went over to the Penn State Library, and Michelle Joseph was there. Not only did she get me a copy of *A Doll's House*, she got me a copy that was annotated with critiques. So I got all kinds of stuff. Did you read?"

I prepare to rattle off my excuse, as if I were in high school again: After an onslaught of media industry layoffs, I'd spent the week in strategic planning sessions with a new leader at my company in Wisconsin. It occurs to me I could milk some brownie points: "Senator McCarthy's home state!" I could fudge, but out here in the real world, I need her grace. So I simply tell her the truth: "I'm about a third of the way through."

A third is even a bit of a stretch. She judges not. "That's okay," she says. "I finished it just a few minutes ago."

It's been twenty-six years since I first read *A Doll's House* in her classroom. The very loose recollection I had of the story was that the antagonist, a male professional of some kind, is very patronizing of his wife, a housewife, and accuses her of having an extramarital affair. I seem to remember that at the end of the story, he decides to forgive her, but by then she cannot unlearn the truth about their marriage: that he does not trust her.

Or something like that.

But as I revisit the first twenty pages, I'm struck at how saccharine the husband Torvald sounds, to the point of condescending his wife, Nora. I make note of his nicknames for her:

My little lark. My little squirrel.

His is their only income, and he reminds her that she is to control what she spends and even what she eats, which is why macaroons were written in as a "vehicle"—a metaphor that appears throughout the story to symbolize a bigger throughline. I think of the macaroons as a way Nora expresses her desire to enjoy life freely and make her own choices, but meanwhile she pretends to oblige her husband by hiding that she's been eating sweets.

Even in 1879, Henrik Ibsen understood that women's bodies are treated as pawns in the argument over basic rights and personal freedom.

"This morning, I'm just going to be your student and your sponge once again," I say.

"Ha!" Mrs. Korthaus laughs. "Okay then, let's get to it."

It's not long before I note that this "lesson" feels different from what I remember of those decades ago when I'd sit captivated as she presented the curriculum. Today I search for her to lead the conversation that same way, but I find that instead she's waiting for me to drive. We're no longer a student and teacher, but more like two thinkers. Equals.

"I didn't teach you *what* to think; I taught you *how* to think," she's said. Now she wants me to show her what I've got. *Work it!*

"Okay, to start: Torvald calls Nora a spendthrift," I reflect. "He tells her overspending 'is like a woman!'"

"Nora is a great character, isn't she? And quite honestly, Torvald Helmer is unfortunately very typical male about a lot of things."

"Our *bodies*," I tell her. "Our *money*. I was writing an article this week and learned that this year marks just fifty years since an American woman could take out a credit card in her own name without her husband's co-signature! And *that* was only fifty years after we gained the right to vote!"

"Which is a very valid observation," Mrs. Korthaus says. "You go back to the late nineteenth century when *A Doll's House* was actually written, and we haven't come that far too quickly, have we? It's really only starting with the Second World War that women were allowed to have a voice, and an opinion, and a place in society."

This is precisely her trademark way of tying in other subjects to the lesson: history, sociology, economics, women's studies. I take advantage of this exchange with her as I've never done before.

"I know you were only a toddler when World War II ended," I tell her, "but why do you think the war was such a turning point for women? Was it because society finally recognized that women could run things if men were absent?"

"I think that's easy to prove, because most of the men had gone off to war. That's where you get Rosie the Riveter: That's when women went to work, and that's how women really got far more responsibility, *and* we became more—not just more responsible, but also more demanding of acknowledgment, and more demanding of just being given credit where we needed it. Oh, yeah. I'm the first generation of that."

It's turning into a thrilling conversation. "Okay then, let me ask you this: In 1974, a woman can finally take out a credit card on her own. You were in your early thirties. I mean, for myself, I spent my twenties in grad school, hardly able to pay my rent in Manhattan. A credit card was my lifeline, not that I managed it well back then. What would you have done in that era of your life?"

"Well, first of all, okay: I have never, ever, ever been trained to handle money. And I hope you are better than I am."

"Self-taught from learning the hard way," I tell her. "But go ahead."

"That was part of the problem, Kris. What the heck?"

Though it was her dad who pushed her to get the most prestigious education available, her mom was the more stable provider while the family simply lived off cash.

"When I went to Pittsburgh for five years to teach at St. Mary of the Mount, I'll never forget: The very, very first thing I realized is that I didn't know how to get a check cashed. I didn't know how to go to a bank. I did not know how to apply for a credit card. Those are the things I had to learn quickly. So I learned—not because I was taught. I learned because I needed to. And you're probably better than I am at things like that. I'm still not good."

"When will the field of education recognize that until we teach girls how to manage that facet of their lives, we will not advance as a society?"

"Correct!"

"It bogs you down with stress and worry. You've seen me on the hamster wheel of my workday to manage the kind of life I want."

"You know what, Kris? The biggest risk in all of that is to be a person like Nora, who finally realizes that all of her inability to handle situations really puts her in the cage—the dollhouse. Nora realizes that her life has been such a sham. She has spent her whole life allowing herself to be manipulated by her husband rather than being honest with him about how she wants to try to stretch herself. So their whole relationship—and I think that's probably true of a lot of women—their relationship is very much affected by the fact that they really haven't been honest with them*selves*, or their spouses, for many things in many ways. She realizes that she has copped out on herself in order to be his doll."

"As women, when we see those red flags, it's so easy to dismiss them until one day your soul is screaming from inside you."

"Oh, wait 'til you get to the end. I learned this morning in the version I read that when Ibsen wrote the play, he had to write two endings to the story."

"He *did*?"

"Yep, I'd never known that before. He recognized that the ending he wanted to give the play wouldn't sit well with audiences. It was too feminist."

"You can spoil it for me. What are the two endings?"

"Okay," she says scrumptiously, as if we're dishing privately about a couple we know. "First you have to remember that years ago Nora borrowed money from Krogstad, the employee whom Torvald ends up firing from the bank. But that money was to pay for Torvald's treatments when he was sick earlier in their marriage. So when Torvald fires Krogstad, Krogstad reveals to Torvald that he'd loaned Nora the money in secret, despite the fact, as Ibsen established early on in the script, that 'a wife could not borrow without her husband's consent.' So throughout the play, Krogstad has blackmailed them, but finally he says, 'I'll forgive you of your debt.' And Torvald basically says, 'Well, isn't this terrific? So now we'll go back to the way our marriage was.'

"But *Nora* sees it differently," she continues. "She says to her husband: 'This is the first time you and I have sat at a table across from one another to have a serious discussion about our personal business.'" Goose bumps ripple up under my yoga pants. "Nora says: 'That's the problem, Torvald. You have treated me like your doll, or your bird,' or whatever the hell he calls her—"

"His little skylark."

"His skylark, that's it. And she responds, 'You don't know me.' He didn't! At this point, Nora has said, 'No flipping way!'" Thirty years later, I'll never *not* love it when she gets fired up. "Essentially, she said, 'I've been mistreated. I have been misinterpreted. I was going to leave you and take my own life, but now I'm not. I'm just going to leave you. I'm going to return to my family home, and I'm going to learn how to be a person. I'm going to learn how to *think*.' He begs her not to, but she leaves him and their kids."

"Nora wants her husband to see her as a capable individual who can autonomously navigate the world."

"Who doesn't, right? So *that* was the first ending," she says.

"And the second?"

"In the second ending, Torvald says, 'You are the mother of my three children. You have to stay because we are a family, and I will change.' That would've been what the public romantics wanted to see happen, right?"

"Yeah, audiences wouldn't have wanted to see her taking off on her kids."

"I think we can assume the correct ending Ibsen intended was for Nora's decision to be, *No, I cannot live with you. I am not the person I want to be. You would never let me grow.* It's kind of interesting that Ibsen knew enough to say that he could not necessarily support that ending. So that's why there are two."

In high school, it had always struck me that Henrik Ibsen, clearly a male playwright, had written this story. In my experience, by the time a writer commits to sit down and write a full work, it's burning inside us and we can tell the idea will not go away. I've always wondered what had inspired him. One difference about relearning this play in 2024 as opposed to in 1997 is that this time, I can turn to Wikipedia.

The gist, as I read it, is that Ibsen had a good friend named Laura who had clandestinely borrowed money to respond to her husband's health problems, and she asked Ibsen if he'd introduce her to his publisher so she could try her hand at getting published with the hope of repaying the debt. He refused, and Laura was ultimately committed to an insane asylum for trying to get her hands on the money, even though she was willing to earn it legitimately. Ibsen felt so guilty and, from what I can gather, saw the inequities women were up against—seriously, being committed for taking on a little debt when men could freely borrow? That was a clear violation of a woman's rights—and decided to tell Laura's story as a work of fiction.

The year 2006 marked a hundred years since Ibsen's death, and records state that *A Doll's House* was still the most performed play in the world. "It surprises me," Mrs. Korthaus says, "that as much as it resonates, there are still men like Torvald. You and I both know them. Q's culture, for instance, is very, very anti-feminine, isn't it?"

The truth is, it makes me uncomfortable when anyone would believe I'd marry a man who's not characteristically kind to women, when, in fact, what drew me to him was the reverence and gentleness and sweetness he showed me, when he spoke of his sister, his mom, his aunts, and even his first wife. I've learned, though, that he is perhaps unique by most standards, not only as a man who grew up Muslim in South Asia.

"His friend's wife, whose marriage was arranged, once told me: 'You understand you have a partner who is not like most other men in our culture, don't you?' I don't think I fully understood that until she said it. He cherishes women; he adores both you and me—I mean, he carried a bowl of oatmeal up here to me in the office this morning because he knew you and I were about to work together and I was busy preparing." People close to me had warned me that if I wanted to meet someone, I shouldn't be too independent; I shouldn't party too much. The person I married loves these traits that make me, me. "He wanted to find someone modern."

"Well," she huffs, "he got quite the sensation in you."

My elementary years were not great and I struggled a lot in school. My parents, and also many of my teachers, kept pushing me and helped me every step of the way. Lasting effects are created through the relationships we educators build with our students. Years from now they may not remember the lessons we taught, but they will remember the times we were there to offer support and encouragement, that we believed in them and supported their dreams, and how we reminded them that anything is possible with hard work and determination.

—Dr. Sheena Smelko, EdD, high school principal
in Pennsylvania (who had walked for her doctorate
graduation ceremony exactly a month
before she shared these thoughts; also the
first woman named as the building principal
at Punxsutawney Area High School)

CHAPTER FOURTEEN

THE TRIBUTES

DID YOU EMAIL ME YOUR QUESTIONS?" MRS. KORTHAUS asks.

Once again I find myself stuttering for an excuse, the way I used to in her classroom when an assignment was late.

I'm a grown woman, and I realize this is the first time I can actually get away with *not* turning something in to her on time. After I moved across the country, I started to model our interview process the way really big celebrities' publicity teams ask us reporters to submit our questions beforehand—first, so they can strike any question that's asking something off-the-record, which is not the case with her; and second, so the figure can prime their thoughts to give the audience intelligent answers.

So before Mrs. Korthaus and I meet, I try to send her a handful of questions I'm hoping we'll discuss. I'd wait for her to say, "No big deal if you don't send them—I mean, hey, it's your project."

But it's not my project. One day in the mail, I receive an envelope. I've always loved the artfully zany quality of her handwriting. When I slice the envelope open, I find a note wrapped inside a tissue like origami:

> *I love our project!*
> *Love,*
> *Carol*

I call her.

"Did you find the hub drive?"

I think she means the thumb drive—but either way, I find it adorable to think how meticulously she'd packaged all this for me. "Let me know what you think when you watch it," she says. "I've been wanting you to see my tributes."

The tributes are a video that was produced when she announced her retirement at age eighty. Students stretching decades back taped themselves sharing their reflections on her impact as a teacher and theater director, and one of my old *Godspell* friends compiled them all into a single video. Then, on closing night of the spring musical the month before she retired, the cast played the video on a giant screen after curtain call.

"Hey, hang— hang on," she says. "Oh shoot." She names another dad whose kids she taught years ago. "He's helping me buy a new car. Let me call you right back."

I plug in the "hub drive" and sit in my office, watching the video on my laptop. The tributes feature many faces I don't recognize, many of them male. Of the past students I can recognize, these old friends of mine went on to enter careers in sales, law, nursing. One was an actor in New York for a time, but found himself a single dad and returned to Pennsylvania to raise his daughter—who appears with him in a duet tribute for Mrs. Korthaus, because his daughter, too, starred in her high school productions.

Even years or decades after graduation, all of them talk about how being led by this giant of a woman brought them to honor a piece of themselves that they hadn't been able to accept. One of the guys makes me pause to rewind and rewatch him. First giving a shy wave to the camera, he says everything: "Mrs. Korthaus, it's Ethan. I only had a small role on the stage, but you played a huge role in my life."

She recently asked me: "Remember how the boys always thought that kind of theater stuff was sissy? They wouldn't come out to sing and dance individually, so I'd pick shows where we needed bigger ensembles so they'd have to all join in together. There have been so many times when we've made the athletes actors. Here's the thing that you have to keep in mind, Kris: If, in fact—if, in *fact*— education works...if, in fact, the principles of faith in education work—if, in *fact*, the humanistic approach to life works—then *you* are, *I* am, ready to take whatever life presents to us. Let me tell you a story. We have a girl at school who is the leading junior bowler in the whole country."

How had I never heard this?

"Well, this morning there was a tournament at the bowling alley, and she asked me to be her partner. Mind you, I've always been part of the ladies' bowling league. I go every Thursday—but to be honest, I'm not a very good bowler. But today? I bowled three of the best games I've ever bowled because I was in the company of very good people. I guess that's how I've lived my life," she says. "I just wanted to get better along the way. Whether it's musicals, whether it's mock trial, I love feeling that people around me have accomplished something. I get tremendous joy in being behind other people's success. Everybody talks about being successful at something. I am very good at making other people look good. And I'm very, very good at making sure things end up being outstanding. I love the feeling of doing that. It's very self-rewarding for me."

I mention the name of a friend I used to star in the school musicals with who today is a stay-at-home mom and whose tribute really struck me. "I liked Elissa's tribute," I tell her.

"What was it?"

"She was holding one of her baby girls, and she said, 'Mrs. Korthaus, when I was an insecure teenage girl, you gave me confidence.'"

"That's another whoa-*ho* moment," Mrs. Korthaus says. "And I love whoa-*ho* moments."

OUR WHOA-*HO* MOMENTS HAVE BECOME HER LEGACY. She taught us the Robert Frost poem "The Road Not Taken," which I remember making a visible impact as we listened around the classroom. When she read out loud for a lesson, she always had a very particular manner of delivery, of emphasizing just the right spots, of taking a beat, of telling the story with her voice, yes, and her hands—but also her diaphragm, her core, her heart. You couldn't *not* pay attention. Listening to her read was more like watching her perform—like being a lucky chosen witness to her own moment of self-discovery:

Two ROADS diverged in a wood...and I—
I took the one LESS traveled by,
And THAT has made ALL the difference.

For a girl who didn't think it was worth trying much of anything, who needed to be challenged not to take the easy path...*she* was all the difference.

"How's the writing coming?" she'd asked me one winter afternoon when I was still back in Pennsylvania and we passed each other in the neighborhood the way we'd both come to count on.

"It's coming." I shrugged. "Just like always. A thousand words a day."

"My God, it's a discipline."

I took, in fact, the hardest path I ever imagined, but now I knew that I could. It's like the golfers and tennis players she's often watching on the TV in her living room when I stop over: Excellence only comes with practice, and committing, over and over, to that practice. For a girl to one day grow and see that she's good at something. To have the confidence in herself to believe she can help move the future forward, in her own way, because someone had shown her that was possible.

If we're in it for the right reasons, we teach, we write, to create a more compassionate world today and a kinder world tomorrow. Mrs. Korthaus listened when I told her what happened when one of the hometown book clubs invited me to speak.

"Well, *I* would just never, *ever*, write a memoir about a small town," said one woman, flicking back her pixie-cut bangs and gingerly yanking up on her popped blouse collar.

"Oh, we both know how she is," Mrs. Korthaus said.

"But you know what? Do you know what's even worse than a book club member who's rude to the author?"

"What?"

"The book club that doesn't read the book."

It's in large part because of what Mrs. Korthaus taught me about perseverance and staying committed to my career for my own sake, about sharing with others what our own lives teach us. There were moments when I felt too self-conscious and exhausted to attend another red carpet and interview more gorgeous celebrities, but I used to tell myself: *If I meet one new contact there, it's worth it.* When I've felt burnt-out and disengaged and still agreed to take on a tough project or go through some industry training, I've told myself: *If I learn one new thing about life, or my career, or my craft, then showing up will have been worth it.* When I meet with a book club, even if everybody's flipping tables and throwing tomatoes because they hate the book, except for one reader who says the book taught them something new or that the story helped them feel that they're not alone, then for me the months of writing a thousand words a day in silence and solitude to be able to show up for that invitation are all worth it.

So next time I take a book club's invitation and they say, "We really read the book!" I will respond: "Good for you." And I'll mean it. Just like voting and opening a bank account weren't attainable for women not long ago, reading a book and discussing ideas aren't guaranteed to every female in the world. These are gifts. What we learn is good for our own minds, and for our children, our students, our future, our civilization.

Our humanity.

I want my students to know that I loved them; that I wanted to share my very real life with them; that I am a good person with good values that they are welcome to imitate; that my life has been so much better because of the students I have worked with.

—**Mrs. Korthaus**

EPILOGUE

"Now remember," she tells me, "I have to run and meet the girls at four thirty."

"How are the girls?"

"Oh, you know. We see each other Mondays and Thursdays and bitch about each other on Tuesdays and Wednesdays."

"I won't keep you." Gosh, her sense of humor is just the best. "I'm just out on a walk; we have some beautiful sun today."

Even three years after her retirement, I am forever scheduling our calls around her mock trial practices, her great-niece's televised basketball games, and dinner dates with the ladies, not to mention the fact that I'm now three hours behind her.

"How are you?" I ask her.

"I feel good!"

I take note that she's started to answer that question this way—it's the first time she's started our conversations by acknowledging her health, which tells me that her illness seems to be on her mind more often. I feel a constant, quiet, nagging guilt about not being there.

"They tell me I have chronic breast cancer," she continues, matter-of-fact. "That's the only way to describe it. A lot of cancers are that way these days, you know? You have a little bit of it and you keep it forever, but the doctors manage it. All my tests keep coming back and it looks like I'm on the right regimen."

In my last few months before the move, I'd watch in her kitchen as she'd take a single dose of a daily pill that keeps the cancer under control. I'm so grateful that if she's sick, it's in the time we're in—and that she's always been so enthusiastic to live her life in a way that kept up with those times.

"Actually," she continues, "right now my arm is hooked up into a system to deaden the part of my brain that's feeling pain. I get this sling off at the end of March, and then after a little bit of physical therapy I should be able to play golf and pickleball again. I don't know whether I'll ever fully return to tennis—but trust me, that won't be any loss to the tennis community."

"Late winter had to be the perfect time of the year to get that taken care of. Hopefully in a few weeks, you'll be able to use it in spring."

"That was the idea! And it's working! Let me tell you what else I'm doing that just came up. The people at Saint Catherine's in our parish asked me to make a presentation this Thursday. I will tell you, or you've probably already figured, my life has been much more contemplative the last few months. I've had time to think, you know? And I certainly have had time to reflect with all of this cancer stuff that I've been doing. Something that's happened that I feel pretty good about is that I've probably gotten closer to my Catholic roots. And you know what else keeps coming up for me?" I could have guessed: "My students."

She says as she reflects on her life, she feels the most peace when she thinks of her faith and her kids. In every conversation when I've asked about her—her life, her stories—every single account led us to a conversation about school, her students, what she taught us, and what we've taught her. I've often had to steer her to talk more about herself because her sights are always on her students.

"Remember I used to talk to you all about becoming 'lifelong learners'? I've always thought of myself that way. I had majored in English, not education. I'd learned how to understand and appreciate literature, and so, therefore, I was teaching you guys because I loved the material so much."

Her ardor for documenting the human experience, and fully living the human experience herself, was contagious. So was her appreciation for feminist works, which I'd probably never have discovered without her at that age.

For every Mrs. Korthaus—for every favorite teacher any one of us still treasures—teaching isn't a job. It's a living profession. Mrs. Korthaus had a way of getting through to us because she was teaching from the perspective of a grown-up who'd intentionally put herself in situations that either thrilled her or challenged her, but in both cases made her wiser, made her stronger, and made her richer in life experience. She still refers to the school as "we" because her work was never about her. I recognize there are thousands of teachers out there who are just as committed to their students as she's been. She loves life. That's why her students love her.

Rejoining with her in my adult years has made us no longer teacher and student. We are peers... contemporaries. She's as much my past, present, and future as my family. Exploring my journey with my great teacher became an opportunity to share what that kind of teacher's love ends up meaning in the future of a child.

The day we carried her patio furniture into the basement for winter, I hugged her in her foyer when I was leaving. That's when I noticed the plant on her entry table—with delicate pine branches and the lightest purple flowers. "Is that real?"

"Sure," she said. "That's a juniper plant. Someone gave it to me after Tom's funeral. It blooms in winter."

I'm not sure why this stayed with me, but a few days later I was still curious enough—curiosity, one of the gifts a good teacher plants in us—to look it up. There it was: Some juniper plants bloom with flowers in the cold months—a hearty plant that can survive the winter, despite how fragile it appears. Science shows it even has a way of communicating with other plants to warn them when harsh weather is coming.

Foreshadowing.

She has done the same. Since my most uncertain years, she has given me the heads-up on what's coming, with the faith that I'd be able to weather it. In my younger years, there were times when her wink and nod in my corner were my only assurance at all. After I'd grown up and met the world on my own and now have asked her to share about her life, just hearing her story is what's given me the knowledge that I can make it through.

I know no one in our community in California, which is not helped by the fact that I work from home, but I've learned how important it is to engage. I volunteer to stand up the sandwich board signs at our entrance's waterfalls to remind our neighbors of the monthly homeowners' meetings. With that role comes a free key to the swimming pool gate to store the signs in the pool house.

At night, I walk down...and I swim. It's just me, the water, and the nightlights that shoot a glow across the floor of the pool. My backstroke and freestyle are nowhere as smooth as they were in third grade, but as my motions slice through the water, I listen to the owls *hoo-hoo*, the crickets sing, the coyotes howl. I float on my back to stare up at the stars, the way the pine trees and palm trees outside the pool fence create a frame around the scene. Every few minutes, a plane flying into or out of SFO blinks its lights red and green. I think of the years I was always coming and going. And I think how thankful I am to now be still. To know who I am, and where I am, in the world.

I have this secret hope that I'll be with her when she leaves this world...that I'll be one of the few with the honor of being present. In times I've had no one, she made sure I had her. She taught me that staying sweet after life's been hard is the bravest thing a woman can do.

Some of us have children to make sure a piece of ourselves stays in the world when we've left. Some of us build buildings. Some of us write books. And some...well, some teach. Mrs. Korthaus never gave birth, but she sure had a lot of kids.

She taught me that to show up in life, I have to engage my mind, my soul, my body, and my community every day. I miss the prayerful, contemplative life at the lake; and on my morning and evening walks with the dogs, I especially miss having her for a neighbor. But in the way I've learned to love myself, to use my mind, and to listen to my heart, I honor my teacher.

When she's gone, may our lives be the proof: Mrs. Korthaus was here. No one can really tell us exactly what's ahead in life...but I'm going to find out.

ACKNOWLEDGMENTS

Teachers, you're our living legends.

It was important to us that a multitude of educators' perspectives were represented in these pages. We didn't reach out to female teachers exclusively, but it was female teachers who responded and made this a book filled with women's voices. Thank you to the following for sharing your reflections on your consequential and powerful role in our world: Brenda Aravich, Wendy Benton, Christine Duplessis, Stephanie Gianni Cochrane, Jessica Green, Tara Kramer, Meghan McBride Connelly, Kelle Pompeii, Mary Mike Sayers (my Miss McEnteer!), Mandi Shick, Heidi Shindledecker, Dr. Sheena Smelko, Mandy Snyder, Nicole Snyder, Tiandra (Snyder) Humes, and Elise O'Brien Tilson. Thank you for bringing your priceless reflections to this book—and most importantly, for the love you put into your work.

I could write memoirs about all the teachers who stand out for having lifted me up so I could get a glimpse of my potential. I have to name at least a few: my Miss Caracciolo, now long known as Mrs. Kathleen Ginther; Sr. Kathryn Preston (I'm every bit as proud of your Principal Awards as I am of my books); Mrs. Barb Stephens; Mrs.

Maureen Kane; Mrs. Janice Kness; Mr. Bill Wright; Mrs. Star Young; Mrs. Lisa Matts; Mr. Joe Ryan; Mrs. Chris Felix (Miss Slaugenhaupt); our beloved departed Lisa Graffius Blasdell; Mr. Jim Murphy; Mrs. Laurie Zamperini; Mrs. Lorraine Ferraraccio; Mrs. Donna Chollock; Mrs. Kate Kunkle; Miss Kathleen Pitrone (now Mrs. Puleo, who made STEAM for girls a thing long before it was); Mr. Mike Nesbit; Mr. Tim O'Connor, Mr. Pat Finn; Mrs. Deb Heigel, Mr. Matt Duffy, Fr. Ed Walk; Fr. Mark Swoger, Mr. Paul Rode; Mrs. Roz Pete, who taught me typing and so much else I carried with me into the world; and the one and only late Mrs. Sophie Lassowsky.

To Tina Lewis, who was also an enlightening figure in the early years of my womanhood.

To Dr. Paul Levinson, who gave me that last vote of confidence I needed before I faced the world, and Dr. Nick Santilli, Dr. Peggy Finucane, Sr. Mary Ann Flannery, Dr. Martin Friedman, and all my instructors at John Carroll. My forever family—go Streaks. Thank you to everyone who guided me at Fordham. Those were profound years of learning.

Thank you to my publishing team at Worthy Books: Jenny Baumgartner for getting it immediately and guiding the way while always keeping the smile in your voice and heaven in your heart, Daisy Hutton, Marissa Arrigoni, Patsy Jones, Cat Hoort, Katie Robison, Becky Maines, Anjuli Johnson, Jen Patten, Laura Essex, and the audio team for your brilliance. I've been a student to all of you. Thank you for sharing your talent and expertise with me.

Thank you, Nena Madonia Oshman (every writer

should have an agent like you), Channy Cornell, Kelly Young, and Brianna McLean—my top-shelf team at the Nominate Group.

Thank you to my colleagues at *Reader's Digest* for your support: Michelle Vartan, Jason Buhrmester, Allison Bean, Jody Rohlena, Miranda Manier, Emily Surpless, Molly Jasinski, Leslie Finlay, Lauren Gray, Tricia Varacallo, Beth Tomkiw.

To the publishing "teachers" who are still my beloved mentors and colleagues: Suzanne Murphy, Suzanne Donahue, Carisa Hays, Dominick Anfuso. Thank you to Michelle Fadlalla Leo and Jodie Cohen—the two best brains (and hearts) in publishing for me to consult for this proposal.

Thank you, Lisa Zocco and Frank Totaro.

To the people in my life who know why I keep going: my husband, Istikram, who is proof that behind a determined woman can only be the strongest kind of man; Jeff and Jennifer; Lori and Mike Skraba; Aunt Becky and Uncle Joe Noelker; Madeline and Marisa; Shayna Ireland; Jacob Yount; Tommy Rubritz; Kyle Morgan; Angie Wingert; Joelle Braid; Lea Ann Heltzel Lonesky; Carrie Linn Branchick; Ross Donadio; Henry Burns; Meghan McBride Connelly; Ashley Peterson; Patrick Connors; Tricia Varacallo; Katie Bressack; Francesca Maxime; Ken Page; Erika Arno; Alex Noya; Bryn Manion; David Yoo; Chuck Lines; Lori Srock.

To Stassi and Dex, whose futures I fight for.

To Mrs. Korthaus: I'd say there's no other teacher like you, but the fact is I know there are thousands. Thank you for letting us into your life so I could try to do just this much to honor them all.

To all the past Central alumni who reached out to me to affirm how special a teacher we all had.

This book is for God. Thank you to my parents for investing in faith education and to my late grandmothers and my teachers for raising me to know and have daily conversations with my Lord. That is the greatest gift anyone can give a child.

ABOUT THE AUTHOR

KRISTINE GASBARRE IS A #1 *NEW YORK TIMES* BEST-selling writer and the author of *How to Love an American Man: A True Story*, as well as the lead editor for The Healthy at *Reader's Digest* (print and digital). Selling nearly a million copies combined, her books have been published in multiple languages and featured in *People*, *The New York Times*, *Rolling Stone*, *Glamour*, NPR, HBO, the Oprah Winfrey Network (OWN), and other international media outlets. She lives with her family in the San Francisco Bay Area, with a home in the Pennsylvania Wilds, and is a passionate volunteer for healthcare equity, women's rights, and animal rescue.